D1552651

SECURE
FOREVER

SECURE FOREVER

HAROLD BARKER

LOIZEAUX BROTHERS
Neptune, New Jersey

FIRST EDITION, JULY 1974
FOURTH PRINTING, APRIL 1986

Library of Congress Cataloging-in-Publication Data

Barker, Harold.
   Secure forever.

   Bibliography: p.
   Includes index.
   1. Assurance (Theology)   2. Perseverance (Theology)
I. Title.
BT785.B37   1986   234   86-7379
ISBN 0-87213-017-7

PRINTED IN THE UNITED STATES OF AMERICA

Dedicated to

LANCE B. LATHAM

"Doc"

from whom I first learned
the glorious truth of
our eternal security in Christ

TRANSLATIONS USED

Authorized King James Version (translated 1611).

American Standard Revised Version. New York: Nelson, 1900.

The New Testament, by Charles B. Williams. Chicago: Moody Press, 1950.

The New Testament in Modern English, by Helen Barrett Montgomery. Philadelphia: Judson Press, 1951.

The Amplified New Testament. Grand Rapids: Zondervan, 1958.

The New Testament — An Expanded Translation, by Kenneth S. Wuest. Grand Rapids: Wm. B. Eerdmans, 1962.

New American Standard Bible — New Testament. Chicago: Moody Press, 1963.

New Scofield Reference Bible. New York: Oxford University Press, 1967.

CONTENTS

INTRODUCTION

Every believer should become acquainted with the doctrine of the eternal security of the believer. Can a truly saved believer ever lose his salvation? We believe that the answer to this question is to be found, not in the reason of man, but in the Word of God. Therefore, the emphasis in this book has been placed upon the Word of God.

This book is not meant to be read as one would read a novel and has not been put together as such, but is meant as an aid in studying the Bible.

Many Christians who believe in the eternal security of the believer know only a few verses to support this belief. One of the purposes of this book is to show the overwhelming weight of Scripture in support of this doctrine. We also intend to show that teaching this doctrine actually brings about in true believers a greater desire to serve the Lord and to grow in the knowledge of Him (just the opposite of what those who deny the security of the believer teach).

The belief of some in the eternal security of the believer is easily shaken by arguments or verses given by those who believe that a saved one may be lost. Another purpose of this book is to answer these arguments from the Word of God.

At the beginning of each section of Part 1 statements are made concerning the eternal security of the believer. Bible verses or passages are then quoted which show the truth of these statements. These verses are quoted from the Authorized King James Version of the Bible. Following these verses are comments and quotations. Other translations of the verses which bring out the meaning more clearly are sometimes quoted. Italics are used to emphasize certain portions of the verses.

In Part 2 arguments against the doctrine of the security of the believer are presented and answered.

In the interest of clearly presenting truth I have drawn freely upon the writings of others. The reader may determine the author quoted, the book, and the page number by checking the note number in the reference notes at the end of the book. All direct quotations are shown by quotation marks.

An index of Scripture references used in this book has also been provided. This should prove especially helpful in finding the answer to passages used to teach that a believer may lose his salvation.

I trust that this book will be a blessing to you and that it will strengthen your belief in the glorious but too often neglected truth of the eternal security of every born-again believer.

HAROLD BARKER

Part 1

THE ETERNAL SECURITY

OF THE BELIEVER

1

THE CLEAR TEACHING OF GOD'S WORD

The "eternal security" of the believer is the clear teaching of God's Word. The following verses state in plain, unmistakable language truths which show that once a person is truly saved he is *secure forever*. In later sections we will examine more carefully some of the truths presented in these verses. Read these verses; believe them; and rejoice in them. Then work for the Lord in the full assurance of your *eternal* salvation, knowing that "your labour is not in vain in the Lord."

> "My sheep hear My voice, and I know them, and they follow Me: And I give unto them eternal life; and they shall never perish, neither shall any man pluck them out of My hand. My Father, which gave them Me, is greater than all; and no man is able to pluck them out of My Father's hand" (John 10:27-29).

This passage states the truth of our security so clearly that none should mistake it. Here is an *unconditional statement* by our Lord Jesus Christ that He *gives* His own (His sheep) *"eternal life"* and that they *"shall never perish,"* and that *no one can take them out of His hand* or *out of His Father's hand*. Why not take these words as they are written and believe them?

One who has *"eternal life"* must be *secure forever;*

One who *"shall never perish"* must be *secure forever;*

One who *cannot be taken out of Christ's hand* or *out of His Father's hand* must be *secure forever!*

13

> "For whom He did foreknow, He also did predestinate to be conformed to the image of His Son, that He might be the firstborn among many brethren. Moreover whom He did predestinate, them He also called: and whom He called, them He also justified: and whom He justified, them He also glorified" (Romans 8:29-30).

Here is a series of truths about every believer. He is *foreknown, predestinated, called, justified, glorified.* If one of these is true of a person, then all are, for they are an unbroken chain.

Everyone foreknown is predestinated.

Everyone predestinated is called.

Everyone called is justified.

Everyone justified is glorified.

What God begins, God finishes! None of these truths are stated as a possible attainment of the believer but all as an already accomplished fact. Even his being glorified is stated in past tense. It is a certainty for everyone who is "foreknown." Therefore, everyone who is "foreknown" (that is every born-again believer) is *secure forever.*

> "Being confident of this very thing, that He which hath begun a good work in you will perform it until the day of Jesus Christ" (Philippians 1:6).

What a wonderful assurance we find in this verse. God not only has "begun a good work" in us but He "will perform it until the day of Jesus Christ." God's performance is not conditioned upon our actions or our continued belief. It is unconditional. He *will* perform it. Therefore, if God has begun a "good work" in you, you are *secure forever.*

> "I know that, whatsoever God doeth, it shall be for ever: nothing can be put to it, nor any thing taken from it: and God doeth it, that men should fear before Him" (Ecclesiastes 3:14).

> "The steps of a good man are ordered by the LORD: and He delighteth in his way. Though he fall, he shall not be utterly cast

down: for the LORD upholdeth him with His hand. For the LORD loveth judgment, and forsaketh not His saints; they are preserved for ever: but the seed of the wicked shall be cut off" (Psalm 37:23-24,28).

This passage is not talking about some who are declared saints after they die but of those on earth who are the Lord's own. They are "preserved for ever."

"Now unto Him that is able to keep you from falling, and to present you faultless before the presence of His glory with exceeding joy" (Jude 24).

When Jesus comes for His own we will stand before God "faultless" because our sin has been taken away at Calvary and His righteousness is counted as ours. We cannot fall from salvation. God won't let us.

"Who shall lay any thing to the charge of God's elect? It is God that justifieth" (Romans 8:33).

God has justified (declared righteous) every believer (His "elect"). Can anyone bring a charge against those whom God has declared righteous?

"For I am persuaded, that neither death, nor life, nor angels, nor principalities, nor powers, nor things present, nor things to come, Nor height, nor depth, nor any other creature, shall be able to separate us from the love of God, which is in Christ Jesus our Lord" (Romans 8:38-39).

For a born-again believer to be lost, he must somehow be separated from the love of God and become an object of God's wrath (John 3:36). These verses make it very clear that absolutely nothing can bring about that separation. To say it is possible to be separated from the love of God and be lost is to deny the intent of these verses. The believer must be *secure forever*.

"But this man, because He continueth ever, hath an unchangeable priesthood. Wherefore He is able also to save them to the uttermost that come unto God by Him, seeing He ever liveth to make intercession for them" (Hebrews 7:24-25).

It is because Jesus "continueth ever" that He is able to save us forever (to the uttermost). The words "to the uttermost" mean "forever." This is shown by the context. He is able to save them "to the uttermost" because He *"ever liveth* to make intercession for them."

> "Neither by the blood of goats and calves, but by His own blood He entered in once into the holy place, having obtained eternal redemption for us" (Hebrews 9:12).

Redemption means to buy by paying a price. Every true believer has been redeemed from the law and its penalty with the blood of Christ (1 Peter 1:18-19; Romans 3:24; Galatians 3:13). Since that is an *"eternal redemption"* we are *secure forever.*

> "For the which cause I also suffer these things: nevertheless I am not ashamed: for I know whom I have believed, and am persuaded that He is able to keep that which I have committed unto Him against that day" (2 Timothy 1:12).

> "Who are kept by the power of God through faith unto salvation ready to be revealed in the last time" (1 Peter 1:5).

If we had to keep our own salvation we would surely lose it, but it is God Himself who keeps us. Surely the true believer can never be lost. He is *secure forever.*

> "And the Lord shall deliver me from every evil work, and will preserve me unto His heavenly kingdom: to whom be glory for ever and ever. Amen" (2 Timothy 4:18).

This verse does not say that this will happen "unless" or "if" or "maybe." The *Lord will preserve me.* I am *secure forever.*

> "And as we have borne the image of the earthy, we shall also bear the image of the heavenly" (1 Corinthians 15:49).

We have borne the image of Adam. Some day we will bear the image of Christ. For every believer this is not just a possibility; it is a certainty!

> "Beloved, now are we the sons of God, and it doth not yet appear what we shall be: but we know that, when He shall appear, we

shall be like Him; for we shall see Him as He is" (1 John 3:2).

Since we can *"know"* that *"we shall be like Him"* we must of necessity be *secure forever.*

"Who shall also confirm you unto the end, that ye may be blameless in the day of our Lord Jesus Christ. God is faithful, by whom ye were called unto the fellowship of His Son Jesus Christ our Lord" (1 Corinthians 1:8-9).

Here again there is no condition placed on the promise: He "shall also confirm you unto the end — blameless." What a wonderful salvation! When Jesus comes for His own we will be *"blameless"* for Christ has taken our sin and He will *confirm us to the end.*

"For ye are dead, and your life is hid with Christ in God. When Christ, who is our life, shall appear, then shall ye also appear with Him in glory" (Colossians 3:3-4).

Where could we find a safer place for our life to be hidden than "with Christ in God"? Is it possible for our salvation to be taken away when it is hidden there? It certainly is not, for verse 4 says that when Christ appears — we *shall* also appear with Him in glory. Our life, our salvation is hidden with Him until then and beyond then even forever.

"For we know that if our earthly house of this tabernacle were dissolved, we have a building of God, an house not made with hands, eternal in the heavens" (2 Corinthians 5:1).

"These things have I written unto you that believe on the name of the Son of God; that ye may know that ye have eternal life, and that ye may believe on the name of the Son of God" (1 John 5:13).

If our salvation could in any conceivable way be lost then this verse does not belong in the Bible for it would be impossible for us to *know* that we have eternal life.

"There is therefore now no condemnation to them which are in Christ Jesus" (Romans 8:1).

In spite of all my sin and shortcomings there is in me "no

condemnation" for I am "in Christ." He has taken my penalty.
"In Christ" I cannot be condemned. I am *secure forever.*

> "According as He hath chosen us in Him before the foundation of
> the world, that we should be holy and without blame before Him in
> love" (Ephesians 1:4).

This is one of the strongest verses I know in support of the
security of the believer. God chose me, not at the end of my life
after He knew I would hold out, but "before the foundation of the
world." Either I am secure forever or God made a mistake in
choosing me.

> "Even when we were dead in sins, hath quickened us together
> with Christ, (by grace ye are saved;) And hath raised us up
> together, and made us sit together in heavenly places in Christ
> Jesus: That in the ages to come He might shew the exceeding
> riches of His grace in His kindness toward us through Christ
> Jesus" (Ephesians 2:5-7).

There is not even a hint of uncertainty here concerning the
future of those who believe. In the ages to come God will be
showing the "exceeding riches of His grace in His kindness
toward us through Christ Jesus." How can we be anything but
secure forever?

> "In whom ye also trusted, after that ye heard the word of truth,
> the gospel of your salvation: in whom also after that ye believed,
> ye were sealed with that holy Spirit of promise, Which is the
> earnest of our inheritance until the redemption of the purchased
> possession, unto the praise of His glory" (Ephesians 1:13-14).

> "And grieve not the holy Spirit of God, whereby ye are sealed
> unto the day of redemption" (Ephesians 4:30).

Since we who know Christ as Saviour are "sealed" with the
Holy Spirit and that "unto the day of redemption," "until the
redemption of the purchased possession," we must be *secure
forever.*

> 'For our conversation [citizenship] is in heaven; from whence
> also we look for the Saviour, the Lord Jesus Christ" (Philippians
> 3:20).

God is so sure of the salvation of us who believe that He has already enrolled us as citizens of Heaven.

> "That whosoever believeth in Him should not perish, but have eternal life. For God so loved the world, that He gave His only begotten Son, that whosoever believeth in Him should not perish, but have everlasting life.... He that believeth on the Son hath everlasting life: and he that believeth not the Son shall not see life; but the wrath of God abideth on him" (John 3 : 15-16 , 36).

If "everlasting life" doesn't last forever then it isn't "everlasting life." If one truly has "everlasting life" he must of necessity be *secure forever.*

> "All that the Father giveth Me shall come to Me; and him that cometh to Me I will in no wise cast out" (John 6 : 37).

> "And this is the Father's will which hath sent Me, that of all which He hath given Me I should lose nothing, but should raise it up again at the last day. And this is the will of Him that sent Me, that every one which seeth the Son, and believeth on Him, may have everlasting life: and I will raise him up at the last day" (John 6 : 39-40).

2

ETERNAL LIFE — OUR PRESENT POSSESSION

In God's Word eternal (everlasting) life is repeatedly spoken of as the *present possession* of the believer (not as some future attainment). It is ours *now*. If one who now possesses eternal life could in any way lose that eternal life then it wasn't eternal! God also says that we may *know* that we have eternal life. If we could lose it in any way we could not *know;* we could only hope.

> "Verily, verily, I say unto you, He that heareth My word, and believeth on Him that sent Me, *hath everlasting life,* and shall not come into condemnation; but is passed from death unto life" (John 5:24).

> *"has eternal life,* and does not come into judgment, but has passed out of death into life" (John 5:24b New American Standard).

> *"possesses eternal life,* and will never come under condemnation, but has already passed out of death into life" (John 5:24b Williams).

This does not say that the believer may someday get eternal life if he holds out, but rather that he *now has it;* he *now possesses it;* he *has already passed out of death into life.* This life which he possesses is *everlasting.* It is *eternal.* If he could ever lose it or throw it away, *it was not everlasting in the first place.*

This verse also says that one who has this everlasting life *"shall not come into condemnation."* If this is true (and it is) then one who has everlasting life can never be lost.

> "He that believeth on the Son hath *everlasting life:* and he that

believeth not the Son shall not see life; but the wrath of God abideth on Him" (John 3:36).

Here again the believer is said to *now have* everlasting life. Some say we can lose it by ceasing to believe. If so then it wasn't everlasting.

"And as Moses lifted up the serpent in the wilderness, even so must the Son of man be lifted up: That whosoever believeth in Him should not perish, but have *eternal life.* For God so loved the world, that He gave His only begotten Son, that whosoever believeth in Him should not perish, but have *everlasting life*" (John 3:14-16).

The word "have" in verses 15 and 16 is in the present tense. The believer now has everlasting life.

"It is a present possession, and is as secure now as it will be ten billion years after we get to Heaven. This is the clear teaching of the Bible, that the work of salvation which is all of the Lord, is a permanent work which shall never fail, since '*He which hath begun a good work in you will perform it until the day of Jesus Christ*' (Philippians 1:6)." [1]

"Verily, verily, I say unto you, He that believeth on Me *hath everlasting life*" (John 6:47).

Here is that same phrase again, "hath everlasting life." If God did not mean it He wouldn't say it.

"These words do not mean a short duration. They do not mean a life for a day, for a month, for a year, nor even for a hundred years; but a life for all of time and for all eternity. If believers have anything, they have "eternal life." For that and that only, is what God purposed and promised, and gives to those who believe on His Son. How simple and how plain is the Word of God!" [2]

"And this is the record, that God hath given to us *eternal life,* and this life is in His Son. He that hath the Son *hath life;* and he that hath not the Son of God hath not life. These things have I written unto you that believe on the name of the Son of God; that ye may *know* that ye have *eternal life,* and that ye may believe on the name of the Son of God" (1 John 5:11-13).

"hath given"— not will give or may give. This is aorist in the Greek, referring to a definite historic act. Something already done.

"hath life" — he now possesses eternal life.

"That ye may *know* that ye have eternal life." We often hear people say that we cannot know whether or not we are going to Heaven until we die. This verse says that we may *know* that we *have* eternal life. We can know *now*. If there were even a remote possibility of losing our salvation it would be impossible to "know." Therefore the believer is eternally secure.

> "Who *hath saved us*, and called us with an holy calling, not according to our works, but according to His own purpose and grace, which was given us in Christ Jesus before the world began" (2 Timothy 1:9).

He "hath saved us." If we have been saved from eternal hell and can somehow be lost again, then we were not really saved from eternal hell but only temporarily detoured.

3

SALVATION NOT OUR DOING

If salvation from the penalty of sin were brought about by our good works and we could lose it by bad works, then we *would* lose it (1 John 1:8). But salvation is *not* brought about by good works and therefore we cannot lose it by our works or lack of them. When a person is relying to any extent on works for salvation from the penalty of sin he hasn't yet clearly seen God's way of salvation.

> "For by *grace* are ye saved through faith; and that *not of yourselves:* it is the *gift of God; Not of works,* lest any man should boast" (Ephesians 2:8-9).

> "For it is *by His unmerited favor* through faith that you have been saved; it is *not by anything that you have done,* it is the gift of God. *It is not the result of what anyone can do,* so that no one can boast of it" (Ephesians 2:8-9 Williams).

> "For it is by *free grace (God's unmerited favor)* that you are saved (delivered from judgment and made partakers of Christ's salvation) through [your] faith. And this [salvation] is *not of yourselves — of your own doing, it came not through your own striving —* but it is the gift of God; *Not because of works [not the fulfillment of the Law's demands],* lest any man should boast. *— It is not the result of what any one can possibly do,* so no one can pride himself in it or take glory to himself" (Ephesians 2:8-9 Amplified Bible).

"This passage deals with the past tense of salvation. It is salvation from the guilt, penalty, and condemnation of sin. *It has already been fully accomplished.* It is *not a process* that is being carried on to be perfected at a later time." [3]

Let's look at this verse a phrase at a time:

"For by grace are ye saved"

Grace is God's *unmerited* favor. It is God doing without asking any price for what He has done. "Grace excludes all merit on the part of the one who is the object thereof. Therefore to be saved by grace cannot take into account any merit in the saved one, either before, at the time of, or after the time he is saved. Furthermore, grace is shown toward the one who is actually guilty. 'While we were yet sinners, Christ died for us' (Romans 5:8). Therefore demerit does not hinder the operation of grace, nor can it set aside that which grace has accomplished. In fact, demerit is the occasion for grace to accomplish its work."[4] "Thus *to be saved by grace is to be unalterably saved and that for all eternity.* The saved one cannot be anything but eternally secure."[5]

" 'By grace are ye saved.' Notice the apostle does not say, 'By grace are ye being saved,' or, 'By grace will ye be saved eventually,' but he is declaring something which is already true of every believer in the Lord Jesus Christ. It is not, 'By grace shall ye be saved if ye abide in the present place,' but 'By grace *are* ye saved,' because the work of redemption is already consummated. Therefore, our salvation is looked at by God as something that is finished and complete. If there were any possibility that somehow along the way to Heaven I might lose the salvation of God, it could not be said that I am already saved, but rather that I am being saved. But, thank God, not only is the work that saves finished, but the salvation is looked upon as an accomplished fact."[6]

The words in the Greek which are translated "are saved" are εστε σεσῳσμένοι. English has no exact equivalent for the construction used here. The word translated "saved" (σεσῳσμένοι) is a perfect, passive, participle. It denotes a condition that is true today because of action in the past that is complete. We "are saved" today because we have been saved completely in the past with the continuing result that we stand saved. Kenneth S. Wuest has a good (but of necessity an awkward) translation in his *Expanded Translation of the New Testament:* "by grace have you been saved in time past completely, through faith, with the result that your salvation persists through present time."

"through faith"

Faith is the means by which we obtain God's salvation. It is not a price we pay, for then salvation could not be by grace. Faith "means a definite taking of one's self out of one's own keeping and entrusting one's self into the keeping of the Lord Jesus."8

"Faith does not only exclude the thought of merit, it actually includes the idea of helplessness and hopelessness. In faith one calls upon another to do that which one is unable to do for oneself. A child in the family is sick and near death. The family physician is called. In so doing the parents confess their own inability to deal with the illness and express their confidence in the doctor. There is no merit in calling the doctor. Their faith in the doctor merely gives him the opportunity to work." 9

"and that not of yourselves"

Not only does God say it is by grace (which excludes any works) and that it is through faith (which is not works) but He adds that it is "not of yourselves." This means we cannot earn salvation nor by our merit keep it, for then it would be of ourselves. "No human merit can contribute to salvation. *God is very zealous to have it known that He and He only is responsible for man's salvation."*10

*"Every argument against the eternal security of the believer is based on the human element. As God definitely and clearly excludes all human element in salvation, every one of these arguments is thereby ruled out."*11

"it is the gift of God"

Salvation is a gift (John 4:10; Romans 5:15; 6:23). If we in any sense could earn our salvation then it would not be a gift.

"not of works"

This is almost a repetition of the phrase "not of yourselves." God wants to make it clear that it is not our doing. If salvation is "by grace then it is no more of works" (Romans 11:6).

"lest any man should boast"

If we could earn our salvation by our works then we could boast, but according to Romans 3:27 boasting is excluded. Boasting in ourselves is excluded by faith in what another,

Christ, has done. We can only glory in Him (1 Corinthians 1:29).

> *"Ye have not chosen Me, but I have chosen you,* and ordained you, that ye should go and bring forth fruit, and that your fruit should remain: that whatsoever ye shall ask of the Father in My name, He may give it you" (John 15:16).

Salvation is of God, not by our works.

> "And if by grace, *then is it no more of works:* otherwise grace is no more grace. But if it be of works, then is it no more grace: otherwise work is no more work" (Romans 11:6).

> "But if it is by His unmerited favor, *it is not at all conditioned on what they have done.* If that were so, His favor would not be favor at all" (Romans 11:6 Williams).

"Here is perhaps the most direct and absolute contrast in Scripture of two principles: for *grace* is God acting sovereignly according to Himself; *works* is man seeking to present to God a human ground for blessing. The two principles are utterly opposed."[12]

> *"Not by works of righteousness which we have done,* but according to His mercy He saved us, by the washing of regeneration, and renewing of the Holy Ghost" (Titus 3:5).

> "He saved us, not on the basis of deeds which we have done in righteousness" (Titus 3:5a New American Standard).

> "not by deeds of uprightness which we performed [in our unsaved state]" (Titus 3:5a Wuest).

> "But *to him that worketh not,* but believeth on Him that justifieth the *ungodly,* his faith is counted for righteousness" (Romans 4:5).

God justifies (declares righteous) the *ungodly.* It is not good people here spoken of, but ungodly people. Works have nothing to do with salvation. If God then declares a man righteous even though he is ungodly, then that man's ungodliness cannot change his standing before God. Ungodly people are the only kind God saves. Until we recognize ourselves as ungodly we cannot be saved.

"Therefore *it is of faith*, that it might be *by grace*; to the end *the promise might be sure* to all the seed; not to that only which is of the law, but to that also which is of the faith of Abraham; who is the father of us all" (Romans 4:16).

The promise is *sure because it is of faith.* If it were of works it would not be sure. Man is always saying, "I must do my part," but if this were necessary the promise could not be sure because man might fail (and would).

"Who hath saved us, and called us with an holy calling, *not according to our works*, but according to His own purpose and grace, which was given us in Christ Jesus before the world began" (2 Timothy 1:9).

If God had called us according to our works, none of us would be called. However, He clearly states He did not call us according to our works.

"For the wages of sin is death; but the *gift of God* is *eternal life* through Jesus Christ our Lord" (Romans 6:23).

A gift is not earned by works. God's gifts will not be taken back. Romans 11:29 says, "For the gifts and calling of God are without repentance."

"But God commendeth His love toward us, in that, *while we were yet sinners, Christ died for us*" (Romans 5:8).

Christ died for us, not because we had repented and turned from our sin, but *"while we were yet sinners."* If we were saved through the death of Christ while "yet sinners," will sin in our lives cause Him to cast us out?

"Therefore *by the deeds of the law there shall no flesh be justified in His sight*: for by the law is the knowledge of sin" (Romans 3:20).

Keeping the law (doing good works) cannot save us. The law can only show us our sin.

"Therefore we conclude that a man is justified by faith *without the deeds of the law*" (Romans 3:28).

"For we reckon that a man is declared righteous by faith, *apart from works of law*"13 (Romans 3:28 Newell).

Here it is plainly stated that justification is *"without"* or *"apart from"* the deeds of the law.

"For we hold that a man is brought into right standing with God by faith, *that observance of the law has no connection with it"* (Romans 3:28 Williams).

"For we hold that a man is justified and made upright by faith *independent of and distinctly apart from good deeds (works of law). — The observance of the Law has nothing to do with justification"* (Romans 3:28 Amplified Bible).

"Knowing that a *man is not justified by the works of the law,* but by the faith of Jesus Christ, even we have believed in Jesus Christ, that we might be justified by the faith of Christ, and *not by the works of the law: for by the works of the law shall no flesh be justified"* (Galatians 2:16).

If a man receives salvation by faith and not by the works of the law (good works), then why is it necessary to keep the law (to keep up good works) in order to keep salvation?

"For as many as are of the works of the law are under the curse: for it is written, Cursed is every one that continueth not in *all* things which are written in the book of the law to do them" (Galatians 3:10).

If one is trying to get salvation by keeping the law this verse shows that he is not saved for he is "under the curse." The law demands absolute perfection and this is impossible. If one can lose his salvation by not keeping the law, then everyone would be lost, for one under the law must continue "in all things which are written in the book of the law to do them." We are not under the law, however, for the believer is "dead to the law" (Galatians 2:19; Romans 7:4).

4

NO CONDEMNATION

The Bible says that for the believer there is "no condemnation"; he "shall never perish"; he "shall not come into condemnation." If one who is truly saved could ever be lost then it would be possible for him to perish; it would be possible for him to come into condemnation. Since God says that this cannot happen the believer must be eternally secure.

> "There is therefore now *no condemnation* to them which are in Christ Jesus" (Romans 8:1).

> "So then there is no condemnation at all for those who are in union with Christ Jesus" (Romans 8:1 Williams).

The remainder of this verse as given in the King James Version is not in the better manuscripts and is omitted in most newer translations.

There is no condemnation to the ones who are "in Christ" or "in union with Christ" because Christ has Himself taken their condemnation at Calvary and therefore "made them free from the law of sin and death" (Romans 8:2).

> "He that believeth on Him *is not condemned:* but he that believeth not is condemned already, because he hath not believed in the name of the only begotten Son of God" (John 3:18).

> "Whoever trusts in Him *is never to come up for judgment;* but whoever does not trust in Him has already received his sentence, because he has not trusted in the name of God's only Son" (John 3:18 Williams).

> "And I give unto them eternal life; and they *shall never perish,* neither shall any man pluck them out of My hand" (John 10:28).

> "And I give them eternal life, and they *shall never lose it or perish throughout the ages* — to all eternity they *shall never by any means be destroyed.* And no one is able to snatch them out of My hand" (John 10:28 Amplified Bible).

> "and I give to them eternal life, and they *shall never get lost,* and no one shall snatch them out of My hand" (John 10:28 Williams).

"They shall never perish." In the Greek text there is a double negative here which intensifies the force of the negative. It could be translated "they shall never, never perish." Wuest translates, "they shall positively not perish, never." The Greek text also adds to this phrase the words which, if translated literally, would read "into the ages" or "forever." "They shall never, never perish forever." When the Lord says that His own shall never perish how can anyone say that it is possible for them to lose their salvation?

"No matter what may befall us in the future; no matter what temptation may beset us; no matter what the works of the Devil; no matter if he throw us down or wallow us in the mire, we do not again 'come into condemnation.' " [14]

> "That whosoever believeth in Him *should not perish,* but have eternal life. For God so loved the world, that He gave His only begotten Son, that whosoever believeth in Him *should not perish,* but have everlasting life" (John 3:15-16).

The believer *will not perish* according to both of these verses. Therefore he must be eternally secure.

> "Verily, verily, I say unto you, He that heareth My word, and believeth on Him that sent Me, hath everlasting life, and *shall not come into condemnation;* but is passed from death unto life" (John 5:24).

> "and *will never come under condemnation,* but has already passed out of death into life" (John 5:24b Williams).

> "and *into judgment he does not come,* but *has been permanently transferred out of the sphere of death* into the life" (John 5:24b Wuest).

If one who believes and as a result "hath everlasting life" could be lost he would have to again come into condemnation. God's Word, however, says he "shall not come into condemnation" or "will never come under condemnation." God's Word is clear. Why not believe it?

"And to wait for His Son from heaven, whom He raised from the dead, even Jesus, which *delivered us from the wrath to come*" (1 Thessalonians 1:10).

Jesus has delivered every one who is saved "from the wrath to come." This verse does not say that "He may deliver us" or that "He will deliver us if we hold out" but states our deliverance as an already accomplished fact.

5

A SURE KNOWLEDGE

It is possible for us to "know" that we have eternal life. If it were possible for a true believer to lose his salvation then such knowledge would be impossible.

> "These things have I written unto you that believe in the name of the Son of God; that ye may *know* that ye have eternal life, and that ye may believe on the name of the Son of God" (1 John 5:13).

> "I write this to you who believe in (adhere to, trust in and rely on) the name of the Son of God — that is, in the peculiar services and blessings conferred by Him on men — so that you may *know* (*with settled and absolute knowledge*) that you [already] have life, yes, eternal life" (1 John 5:13 Amplified Bible).

We could not possibly have such a knowledge if there were any chance whatever that we might lose that eternal life.

> "Beloved, now are we the sons of God, and it doth not yet appear what we shall be: but we *know* that, when He shall appear, we shall be like Him; for we shall see Him as He is" (1 John 3:2).

For us to *know* that "we shall be like Him" would also be impossible if we could lose our salvation.

> "For we *know* that if our earthly house of this tabernacle were dissolved, we have a building of God, an house not made with hands, eternal in the heavens" (2 Corinthians 5:1).

Can one who has the possibility of losing his salvation say that he *knows* that he has "a building of God, an house not made with hands, eternal in the heavens"?

"Therefore, my beloved brethren, be ye stedfast, unmoveable, always abounding in the work of the Lord, forasmuch as ye *know* that your labour is not in vain in the Lord" (1 Corinthians 15:58).

Only one who is eternally secure could truly *"know"* that his *"labour is not in vain in the Lord."* If he could lose his salvation his labor *would be* in vain. This verse comes at the end of a passage which is looking forward to the rapture of the Church. Can one who might lose his salvation look forward with confidence and *know* that when Jesus comes to catch up His own his labor is not in vain?

"*Knowing* that He which raised up the Lord Jesus shall raise up us also by Jesus, and shall present us with you" (2 Corinthians 4:14).

"because I *know* that He who raised the Lord Jesus from the dead will raise me too in fellowship with you" (2 Corinthians 4:14 Williams).

This verse speaks of the fact that Jesus shall raise us up as sure knowledge. Paul *knows* that this will happen not only to himself but also to the believers to whom he was writing. Is such knowledge possible if we could lose our salvation?

6

A NEW CREATION

The Bible says that one who is "in Christ" is a "new creature" (creation). His body is not a "new creation," nor is his mind, but spiritually he is a "new creature." He has a new nature. It is understandable that a creature which has been brought into a new environment or has been taught new tricks will occasionally return to its old habits and way of life. Its nature is still the same. For example: a dog may be taught to walk only on its hind legs, but no matter how long its period of training or how good its teacher, it will still occasionally walk on all fours. This is its nature.

A "professing" Christian who has not really been saved may change his habits and acquire new ones. He may go to church and find new friends but his nature is still the same and eventually it will show itself. However one who has really been saved has a new nature; he is a new creation; "old things are passed away; behold, all things are become new." He may occasionally slip into sin but he will not be happy nor will he "continually practice sin" for he has a new nature.

> "Therefore if any man be in Christ, he is *a new creature:* old things are passed away; behold, all things are become new" (2 Corinthians 5:17).

> "So if anybody is in union with Christ, he is the work of a new creation; the old condition has passed away, a new condition has come" (2 Corinthians 5:17 Williams).

A "creation" is something that *is made.* It does not make itself, nor can it change itself into something else. Therefore, since everyone who is "in Christ" (those who are born-again believers) is a "new creation" he cannot change himself into something else. Neither can he kill the new creation and raise it again. If a truly saved believer can be lost and saved again this would have to happen.

"For in Christ Jesus neither circumcision availeth any thing, nor uncircumcision, but *a new creature*" (Galatians 6:15).

"For neither is circumcision [now] of any importance, nor uncircumcision, but [only] *a new creation* [the result of a new birth and a new nature in Christ Jesus, the Messiah]" (Galatians 6:15 Amplified Bible).

"For we are His workmanship, *created in Christ Jesus* unto good works, which God hath before ordained that we should walk in them" (Ephesians 2:10).

"For He has made us what we are, because He has *created us through our union with Christ Jesus* for doing good deeds which He beforehand planned for us to do" (Ephesians 2:10 Williams).

"And that ye put on the *new man,* which after God *is created* in righteousness and true holiness" (Ephesians 4:24).

"and that you *have put on once for all the new self* who after God was created in righteousness and holiness of truth" (Ephesians 4:24 Wuest).

"The 'new man' is the regenerate man as distinguished from the old man (Romans 6:6), and is a new man as having become a partaker of the divine nature and life (Colossians 3:3-4; 2 Peter 1:4), and in no sense the old man made over, or improved (2 Corinthians 5:17; Galatians 6:15; Ephesians 2:10; Colossians 3:10)."[15]

"I can thoroughly understand how the dog would return to his vomit (2 Peter 2:22), simply because he remained a dog. His nature is unchanged. But I cannot understand how a genuinely regenerated man can talk of taking his fill of sin. I can thoroughly understand how the raven, sent out by Noah, didn't return to the ark (Genesis 8:7). He did not need to return. Everywhere was food for his raven nature. He could feast and feast to his heart's content. The whole surface of the waters was covered with dead bodies overwhelmed in the flood. Again, I can thoroughly understand why the dove did return to the ark (Genesis 8:8-9). He could not eat carrion — he did not love carrion — he must return to the ark. Many a man who simply professes conversion can go out into the world and be satisfied to stay. He still has his raven nature. He can with content and pleasure feast upon sin. Not so, however, the genuinely converted. His nature has been changed. He may go into sin. Led by the terrible tempter, he may go far astray. He, however, will never be at ease. Never be satisfied. Like the dove he will find no genuine rest for the sole of his foot. His new nature will revolt at sin. He will always long to come back." 16

7

SONS OF GOD BY NEW BIRTH (REGENERATION)

Every true believer has been "born again." He is a "son of God." He has been born into the family of God spiritually. If you have truly been "born again" you are a son of God. God will in love "chasten" you, even as we "chasten" or punish our children when they disobey, but you will always be in His family. He will never cast you out.

> "Being *born again*, not of corruptible seed, but of *incorruptible*, by the word of God, which liveth and abideth for ever" (1 Peter 1:23).

> "for you have been *born again* not of seed which is perishable but *imperishable*, that is, through the living and abiding word of God" (1 Peter 1:23 New American Standard).

The true believer has already been "born again." Corruptible seed can die, but we have been born again "not of corruptible seed, but of incorruptible." Incorruptible means that it *cannot die*. Since the saved one has been born again of incorruptible seed he cannot be lost.

> "Jesus answered and said unto him, Verily, verily, I say unto thee, Except a man be *born again*, he cannot see the kingdom of God" (John 3:3).

> "Jesus answered him, 'I most solemnly say unto you, no one can ever see the kingdom of God, unless he is *born from above'* " (John 3:3 Williams).

The *New Scofield Bible* note on regeneration says,

"Regeneration: (1) The necessity of the new birth grows out of the incapacity of the natural man to 'see' or 'enter into' the kingdom of God. However gifted, moral, or refined he may be, the natural man is absolutely blind to spiritual truth and impotent to enter the kingdom; for he can neither obey, understand, nor please God (v.3,5-6; cp. Ps. 51:5; Jer. 17:9; Mk. 7:21-23; 1 Cor. 2:14; Rom. 8:7-8; Eph. 2:3. See Mt. 6:33). (2) The new birth is not a reformation of the old nature (Rom. 6:6), but a creative act of the Holy Spirit (Jn. 3:5; cp. 1:12-13; 2 Cor. 5:17; Eph. 2:10; 4:24). (3) The condition of the new birth is faith in Christ crucified (Jn. 3:14-15; cp. 1:12-13; Gal. 3:24). (4) Through the new birth the believer becomes a member of the family of God (Gal. 3:26; 1 Pet. 1:23) and a partaker of the divine nature, the life of Christ Himself (Gal. 2:20; Eph. 2:10; 4:24; Col. 1:27; 2 Pet. 1:4; 1 Jn. 5:10-12). And (5) in view of Ezek. 36:25-26, Nicodemus should have known about the new birth. Observe the correspondence between the 'clean water,' the 'new spirit,' and the 'new heart' of the Ezekiel passage with the 'water,' 'Spirit,' and new birth ('born again') of Jn. 3:5, 7." [17]

"That which is *born of the flesh is flesh:* and that which is *born of the Spirit is spirit*" (John 3:6).

"To be saved does not mean that this life which is born of the flesh is changed or made over. This cannot happen, for its nature cannot be changed. That is the condition that makes the new birth imperative. The only thing God could do with the flesh was to judge it, and the judgment resulted in condemnation and execution (Romans 8:3; Galatians 2:19; Romans 6:6).

"The new birth is a birth of the Spirit. It is to be 'born, not of blood, nor of the will of the flesh, nor of the will of man, but of God' (John 1:13). *It is the coming into being of a new, divine life which has the incorruptible and immortal (not subject to death) nature of God.*" [18]

"Water never rises above its level; that which is produced is of the same nature as that which produces. We find people today who think that if they were in other circumstances they would have a better chance of getting saved. The rich man thinks that if he were poor, he might have time to think of religion. The poor man thinks that if he could get ends to meet and had a little more money he would have more leisure to think of God. But the difficulty is not so much in what is *around* us, as in what is *within* us."[19]

Most religion is just "cultivating the flesh."[20]

A human being is born a human being and cannot by his "freewill" make himself into a dog even though he greatly desires to be one. Since "that which is born of the Spirit is spirit" then a born-again believer cannot by exercising his "freewill" make himself something else. A truly born-again believer would not really want to be anything else!

> "But as many as received Him, to them gave He power to become the *sons of God*, even to them that believe on His name: Which *were born*, not of blood, nor of the will of the flesh, nor of the will of man, *but of God*" (John 1:12-13).

Those who know Christ as Saviour are "sons of God." They have by *"new birth"* become part of God's family. Since this "new birth" was "of God" and not "of the will of the flesh, nor of the will of man," how can man undo what God has done?

> "Not by works of righteousness which we have done, but according to His mercy He saved us, by the washing of regeneration, and renewing of the Holy Ghost" (Titus 3:5).

> "He saved us, not because of any works of righteousness that we had done, but because of His own pity and mercy, by [the] cleansing (bath) of the new birth (regeneration) and renewing of the Holy Spirit" (Titus 3:5 Amplified Bible).

"The nature of the work of regeneration forbids any possible human assistance. As a child in natural birth is conceived and born without any volition on his part, so the child of God receives the new birth apart from any volition on his part. In the new birth, of course, the human will is not opposed to regeneration and wills by divine grace to believe, but this act in itself does not produce new birth. As in the resurrection of the human body from physical death, the body in no way assists the work of resurrection, so in the work of regeneration, the human will is entirely passive. It is not that the human will is ruled aside, nor does it waive the human responsibility to believe. It is rather that regeneration is wholly a work of God in a believing heart."[21]

"One of the many reasons for the confusion in the doctrine of regeneration is the attempt to avoid the inevitable conclusion that a soul once genuinely regenerated is saved forever. The bestowal of eternal life cannot be revoked. It declares the unchangeable purpose of God to bring the regenerated person to glory. Never in the Scriptures do we find anyone regenerated a second time. While Christians may lose much of a normal spiritual experience through sin, and desperately need confession and restoration, the fact of regeneration does not change."[22]

> "The Spirit itself beareth witness with our spirit, that we are the *children of God:* And if *children,* then *heirs; heirs of God,* and *joint-heirs* with Christ; if so be that we suffer with Him, that we may be also glorified together" (Romans 8:16-17).

> "Wherefore thou art no more a servant, but *a son*; and if a son, then an *heir of God* through Christ" (Galatians 4:7).

> "For ye are all the *children of God* by faith in Christ Jesus" (Galatians 3:26).

We are "sons of God"

"heirs of God"

"joint-heirs with Christ"

"Will the Father disinherit us? If we had been taken into His family because of some merit in us, then He might. But Christ, His own beloved Son, brought the whole thing about. It was for His sake that we were taken into the family of God. While Christ remains true to His younger brothers and sisters, there will be no disinheritance. If this thing fails, then either God or Christ will have to fail. It would indeed be our misfortune, our loss, our condemnation, but it would be God's failure. Without anything to commend us, He adopted us. He made us His heirs and joint heirs with His Son. Beloved, I am persuaded that there will be no failure."[23]

> "For whom the Lord loveth He chasteneth, and scourgeth every son whom He receiveth. If ye endure chastening, God dealeth with you as with sons; for what son is he whom the father chasteneth

not? But if ye be without chastisement, whereof all are partakers, then are ye bastards, and not sons" (Hebrews 12:6-8).

"For the Lord corrects and disciplines every one whom He loves, and He punishes, even scourges, every son whom He accepts and welcomes to His heart and cherishes. You must submit to and endure [correction] for discipline. God is dealing with you as with sons; for what son is there whom his father does not [thus] train and correct and discipline? Now if you are exempt from correction and left without discipline in which all [of God's children] share, then you are illegitimate offspring and not true sons [at all]. [Proverbs 3:11-12]" (Hebrews 12:6-8 Amplified Bible).

As any good father, God chastens (corrects and disciplines) His own children. He does this because He loves us. He does not cast us out of His family because of sin but punishes us now, in this life, to bring us back into His will (1 Corinthians 11:29-32).

"Think for a moment. Did Jesus speak the truth or tell lies? If He spoke truth, those who have not *been born again* — however intelligent, educated, moral, benevolent, or religious — can never see the kingdom of God, and must, therefore, be swept away forever with the lost, for there are only two places."[24]

"The awful fact remains. Stop therefore, high or low, rich or poor, educated or uneducated, intelligent or ignorant, religious man or blasphemer, respectable or profane, think, and ask yourself these questions: *Am I born again? Have I a new life* — a life communicated by the Spirit of God through the truth — born not of flesh, but of water (the Word, Ephesians 5:26) and of the Spirit? *Have I been born twice* — once into this world of Adam and again into that of God? Friend, if you have not this new birth, it were better that you had never been born. Now, as you are, and where you are, whenever you are convinced of the necessity of this new birth, look and live; believe and be saved; take God at His word. He says 'Ye *must* be born again,' and in the same chapter it is written, 'As Moses lifted up the serpent in the wilderness, even so *must* the Son of man be lifted up. That whosoever *believeth* in Him should not perish, but have *eternal life.*' — What God demands, God provides."[25]

8

CITIZENS OF HEAVEN

All who truly know Christ as their Saviour are already *"citizens" of Heaven.* This world is not our home. Could God have made a mistake in making us citizens of Heaven? We have not yet reached Heaven but it is already our "home," our "citizenship" is already there. Someday we *will* be there too!

> "Now therefore ye are no more strangers and foreigners, but *fellowcitizens with the saints,* and *of the household of God"* (Ephesians 2:19).

> "Therefore you are no longer outsiders — exiles, migrants, and aliens, excluded from the rights of citizens; but you now share *citizenship* with the saints — God's own people, consecrated and set apart for Himself; and you belong to God's [own] household" (Ephesians 2:19 Amplified Bible).

> "For *our conversation is in heaven;* from whence also we look for the Saviour, the Lord Jesus Christ" (Philippians 3:20).

The word here translated "conversation" would be much better translated "citizenship":

"Our citizenship is in heaven" (American Standard Revised)

"Our commonwealth is in heaven" (Montgomery)

"We are citizens of the state (commonwealth, homeland) which is in heaven" (Amplified Bible)

"the commonwealth of which we are citizens has its fixed location in heaven" (Wuest).

"For *we know* that if our earthly house of this tabernacle were dissolved, we have a building of God, *an house not made with hands, eternal in the heavens*" (2 Corinthians 5:1).

If we can *know* that *heaven is our eternal home* (and we can), then we cannot lose our salvation.

"But ye are come unto mount Sion, and unto the city of the living God, the heavenly Jerusalem, and to an innumerable company of angels, To the *general assembly and church of the firstborn, which are written in heaven,* and to God the Judge of all, and to the spirits of just men made perfect" (Hebrews 12:22-23).

"And to the church (assembly) of the First-born who *are registered [as citizens] in heaven*" (Hebrews 12:23a Amplified Bible).

"to the festal gathering and assembly of God's first-born sons *enrolled as citizens in heaven*" (Hebrews 12:23a Williams).

Every born-again believer is already registered (enrolled) as a citizen of Heaven. Is it possible that God made a mistake in registering me? If I could lose my salvation, He did.

9

THINGS THAT SHALL BE

In the following verses, there is no question about whether or not certain things will be so. It is plainly stated that they "shall" be! It is not said that these things "may" be or that they are "possible," nor is it stated that they are "probable." They "shall" be!

> "When Christ, who is our life, shall appear, then *shall* ye also appear with Him in glory" (Colossians 3:4).

There are no "if's" or "maybe's" here. This is definite. Those to whom Paul was writing, that is, all those "in Christ" at Colosse, would appear with Christ in glory. This would, of course, apply to all those "in Christ" everywhere, as well as those at the city of Colosse. *If you are "in Christ" you "shall" appear with Him in glory.*

> "But God commendeth His love toward us, in that, while we were yet sinners, Christ died for us. Much more then, being now justified by His blood, we *shall* be saved from wrath through Him" (Romans 5:8-9).

> "But God proves His love for us by the fact that Christ died for us while we were still sinners. So if we have already been brought into right standing with God by Christ's death, *it is much more* certain that *by Him* we *shall be* saved from God's wrath"(Romans 5:8-9 Williams).

If you have been saved from the penalty of your sin through what Christ did for you at Calvary, God says that it is *even more certain* than this that you "shall" be saved from God's wrath.

> "For if by one man's offence death reigned by one; much more they which receive abundance of grace and of the gift of righteousness *shall* reign in life by one, Jesus Christ" (Romans 5:17).

If you have received God's "gift of righteousness," which is to say, "if you are saved" then you *"shall* reign"!

> "But if the Spirit of Him that raised up Jesus from the dead dwell in you, He that raised up Christ from the dead *shall* also quicken your mortal bodies by His Spirit that dwelleth in you " (Romans 8:11).

Since the Holy Spirit dwells in all who are saved (Romans 8:9) and the Spirit "shall" quicken (make alive) the mortal (subject to death) bodies of all in whom He dwells, then all who are saved "shall" be quickened (made alive). This is looking forward to the bodily resurrection of all believers.

> "For I reckon that the sufferings of this present time are not worthy to be compared with the glory which *shall* be revealed in us" (Romans 8:18).

Is the Apostle Paul attempting to mislead the Christians at Rome into a false security? If it is possible for one to lose his salvation shouldn't he have said, "the glory which may perhaps be revealed in us if we don't lose our salvation"?

> "Who *shall* also confirm you unto the end, that ye may be blameless in the day of our Lord Jesus Christ" (1 Corinthians 1:8).

> "and to the very end He *will guarantee* that you are vindicated at the day of our Lord Jesus Christ"(1 Corinthians 1:8 Williams).

Can a truly saved one be lost when God *guarantees* that he will be vindicated?

> "And as we have borne the image of the earthy, we *shall* also bear the image of the heavenly" (1 Corinthians 15:49 Williams).

This was written to those who were saved at Corinth and "in every place" (1 Corinthians 1:2). "We shall" bear the "image of the heavenly." If you are saved do you *still* have doubts?

"Behold, I shew you a mystery; We shall not all sleep, but we *shall* all be changed" (1 Corinthians 15:51).

When Jesus comes to catch up His own, all who are truly saved *"shall" be* changed whether they are dead or alive.

"Knowing that He which raised up the Lord Jesus *shall* raise up us also by Jesus, and *shall* present us with you" (2 Corinthians 4:14).

"Assured that He Who raised up the Lord Jesus will raise us up also with Jesus and bring us [along] with you into His presence" (2 Corinthians 4:14 Amplified Bible).

"Beloved, now are we the sons of God, and it doth not yet appear what we shall be: but we *know* that, when He shall appear, we *shall* be like Him; for we shall see Him as He is" (1 John 3:2).

There is no uncertainty here: *"we know — we shall be like Him."*

10

KEPT BY GOD

The Scriptures clearly teach that salvation from the penalty of sin is a gift of God. We cannot earn it. We can only in faith accept it. The Scriptures also teach that, once this salvation is ours, *God will keep us.* If salvation is of God and He says that He will keep us, then He will! For us to lose our salvation would mean that God had failed.

> "Being confident of this very thing, that He which hath begun a good work in you *will perform it until the day of Jesus Christ"* (Philippians 1:6).

God began the work. *He* will perform it. "Because salvation is of the Lord, it must endure. Because He is the Author of our faith (Hebrews 12:2), He must be the Finisher as well."[26]

> "For ye are dead, and *your life is hid with Christ in God"* (Colossians 3:3).

He keeps our life. It is hidden with Him.

> "What shall we then say to these things? If God be for us, who can be against us? He that spared not His own Son, but delivered Him up for us all, how shall He not with Him also freely give us all things?" (Romans 8:31-32)

Why should God be "for us" enough to save us when we were undeserving hell-bound sinners, and then turn against us after we are His born-again children? Would He have paid such a price if He knew beforehand that He would not keep us? God has already paid the supreme price, "He ... spared not His own Son." Will He not now "freely give us all things?"

> "But this man, because He continueth ever, hath an unchangeable priesthood. Wherefore *He is able also to save them to the uttermost* that come unto God by Him, seeing He ever liveth to make intercession for them" (Hebrews 7:24-25).

The word translated "uttermost" means "completely" or "thoroughly." This same word is translated "unto the end" in John 13:1.

"It is not that Christ is able to reach utterly bad cases, although that is true; but that He is able to carry the believer right through all trials, temptations, and infirmities, unto the completion of his pilgrimage, and present him faultless in the day of His coming again." [27]

"He is able to save *to the completion*" (Newberry)

"He is able to save *completely*" (Williams)

"He is able to save *forever*" (New American Standard)

"He is able also to save to the *uttermost — completely, perfectly, finally, and for all time and eternity*" (Amplified Bible)

Dr. H. A. Ironside writes: "It should be noted that salvation to the uttermost here does not simply mean salvation from every kind of sin, but is even greater than that — salvation forevermore. He whom God saves is saved eternally, for He who died for him lives to keep him and to complete the work He began." [28]

> "Let your conversation be without covetousness; and be content with such things as ye have: for He hath said, *I will never leave thee, nor forsake thee*" (Hebrews 13:5).

> "I will in no wise fail thee, neither will I in any wise forsake thee" (Hebrews 13:5b American Standard Revised).

> "Who shall separate us from the love of Christ? shall tribulation, or distress, or persecution, or famine, or nakedness, or peril, or sword? As it is written, For Thy sake we are killed all the day long; we are accounted as sheep for the slaughter. Nay, in all these things we are more than conquerors through Him that loved us.

For I am persuaded, that neither death, nor life, nor angels, nor principalities, nor powers, nor things present, nor things to come, Nor height, nor depth, nor any other creature, shall be able to separate us from the love of God, which is in Christ Jesus our Lord" (Romans 8:35-39).

In John 3:36 we are told that the "wrath of God" abides on those who believe not the Son.

"If it be possible for one who has been saved to be lost, it must of necessity be possible for one who has been the object of the love of God to be taken out of that position and be made the object of the wrath of God."[29] This cannot happen since we are shown in no uncertain terms in Romans 8:35-39 that *nothing* can separate us from the love of God.

"If anything is emphatically taught in the Bible, it is that when man has become the object of the everlasting love of God, there is no change in that condition."[30]

How much plainer can God make it? "Can you think of anything which is not included in this category: death, life, angels, principalities, powers, things present and future, height nor depth. It includes everything in Heaven and earth and hell, now and in the future, but among them all not a thing can be found which can separate us from the love of God in Christ Jesus."[31]

"And this is the Father's will which hath sent Me, that of all which He hath given Me *I should lose nothing,* but *should raise it up again at the last day.* And this is the will of Him that sent Me, that every one which seeth the Son, and believeth on Him *may have everlasting life: and I will raise him up at the last day"* (John 6:39-40).

It is the Father's will that Christ should lose none of those which the Father has given Him. Jesus says that He will raise him up at the last day. Do we need more assurance than the word of Christ?

The word "may" in verse 40 does not indicate any uncertainty. Williams translates, "shall have everlasting life, and I shall raise him to life on the last day."

"No man can come to Me, except the Father which hath sent Me draw him: and *I will raise him up at the last day*" (John 6:44).

Only those whom the Father "draws" can come to Christ, and Jesus says that He will raise these. If a person is not raised up at the last day it is because he never came to Christ.

"And now I am no more in the world, but these are in the world, and I come to Thee. Holy Father, *keep through Thine own name those whom Thou hast given Me,* that they may be one, as We are" (John 17:11).

Jesus is praying and asks that the Father keep those which He has given Him. Since Jesus is certainly praying according to the will of the Father His prayer will be answered.

"Neither pray I for these alone, but for them also which shall believe on Me through their word; That they all may be one; as Thou, Father, art in Me, and I in Thee, that they also may be one in Us: that the world may believe that Thou hast sent Me" (John 17:20-21).

Jesus here extends His prayer to include all believers since His disciples, as well. *"If a single saved person becomes lost, this prayer is not fully answered."*[32]

"For by one offering *He hath perfected for ever* them that are sanctified" (Hebrews 10:14).

"The *once* of Christ's work is the secret of it being *forever.*"[33] The sacrifices of the Old Testament could not make the worshipers perfect and therefore had to be offered continually (Hebrews 10:1-3). But Christ's sacrifice *was* perfect and has *"perfected for ever* them that are sanctified." One perfect sacrifice was enough and does not need to be offered after each new sin.

Can those who have been *"perfected for ever"* be lost?

"For the gifts and calling of God are *without repentance*" (Romans 11:29).

"for the gracious gifts and call of God are *never taken back*" (Romans 11:29 Williams).

"For God's gifts and His call are irrevocable — He never withdraws them when once they are given, and He does not change His mind about those to whom He gives His grace or to whom He sends His call" (Romans 11:29 Amplified Bible).

Eternal life is a *gift* of God (Romans 6:23; John 10:28).

Salvation is a *gift* of God (Ephesians 2:8).

Righteousness is a *gift* of God (Romans 5:16-17).

The *Holy Spirit* is a *gift* of God (1 Thessalonians 4:8).

According to Romans 11:29 God will not take back or withdraw these gifts. Since all who are truly saved *now* have these gifts, *they will always have them.*

"If God says that He does not repent having given a gift, it is contradicting Him and making Him a liar to say that He takes His gifts back."[34]

"I thank my God always on your behalf, for the grace of God *which is given you by Jesus Christ; That in every thing ye are enriched by Him,* in all utterance, and in all knowledge; Even as the testimony of Christ was confirmed in you: So that *ye come behind in no gift;* waiting for the coming of our Lord Jesus Christ. *Who shall also confirm you unto the end, that ye may be blameless in the day of our Lord Jesus Christ. God is faithful,* by whom ye were called unto the fellowship of His Son Jesus Christ our Lord" (1 Corinthians 1:4-9).

It is hard to believe that this is written concerning the same people about whom it is said:

"Ye are yet carnal" (1 Corinthians 3:3)

"There is fornication among you (1 Corinthians 5:1)

"There are contentions among you" (1 Corinthians 1:11)

"Brother goeth to law with brother" (1 Corinthians 6:6)

"There are divisions among you" (1 Corinthians 11:18)

But it *is* written concerning them and *in the same letter:*

"In every thing ye are enriched by Him"

"Ye come behind in no gift"

"Ye may be blameless in the day of our Lord Jesus Christ"

How can these things be said about sinful men, which some would say are in danger of being lost? The answer is because of "the grace of God" (1 Corinthians 1:4), because God is faithful (1:9), and because Christ shall confirm them unto the end (1:8).

Notice especially what is said in 1 Corinthians 1:8 about His keeping us:

> "and to the very end He will guarantee that you are vindicated at the day of our Lord Jesus Christ" (1 Corinthians 1:8 Williams).

> "And He will establish you to the end — keep you steadfast, give you strength, and guarantee your vindication, that is, be your warrant against all accusation or indictment — [so that you will be] guiltless and irreproachable in the day of our Lord Jesus Christ, the Messiah" (1 Corinthians 1:8 Amplified Bible).

> "All that the Father giveth Me shall come to Me; and him that cometh to Me I will *in no wise cast out*" (John 6:37).

> "Everyone whom the Father gives Me will come to Me; and him who comes to Me I will *never reject*" (John 6:37 Montgomery).

> "All that the Father gives to Me shall come to Me, and the one who comes to Me *I will positively not throw out into the outside*" (John 6:37 Wuest).

Some say that Christ will reject us or cast us out if we don't hold out. Christ says, "I will *in no wise cast out*," "I will *never reject.*" Who is correct?

> "Blessed be the God and Father of our Lord Jesus Christ, which according to His abundant mercy *hath* begotten us again unto a lively hope by the resurrection of Jesus Christ from the dead, *To an inheritance incorruptible, and undefiled, and that fadeth not away, reserved in heaven for you,* Who are *kept by the power of God* through faith unto salvation ready to be revealed in the last time" (1 Peter 1:3-5).

We have an inheritance *reserved* in Heaven. It is God who has reserved it for us. Did He make a mistake in reserving it for us? How can He "reserve" anything for us if there is a possibility that we might be lost? The truth is that He can reserve it for us for *He keeps us. We are "kept by the power of God."*

"protected by the power of God' (New American Standard);

"guarded (garrisoned) by God's power" (Amplified Bible).

"For the which cause I also suffer these things: nevertheless I am not ashamed: *for I know* whom I have believed, and am persuaded that He *is able to keep that which I have committed unto Him against that day*" (2 Timothy 1:12).

"for I know whom I have trusted and I am absolutely sure that He is able to *guard what I have intrusted to Him until that day*" (2 Timothy 1:12 Williams).

Expositor's Greek Testament says: "*that which I have deposited for safe keeping.*" [35]

What have we committed to Him for safekeeping? Our salvation, our souls, ourselves, our eternal future!

"And the *Lord shall deliver me from every evil work, and will preserve me* unto His heavenly kingdom: to whom be glory for ever and ever. Amen" (2 Timothy 4:18).

It is the Lord that delivers us and preserves us.

"But the Lord is faithful, who shall stablish you, and keep you from evil" (2 Thessalonians 3:3).

It is the Lord that keeps us.

"Now unto Him that is able to keep you from falling, and to present you faultless before the presence of His glory with exceeding joy, To the only wise God our Saviour, be glory and majesty, dominion and power, both now and ever. Amen" (Jude 24-25).

We do not keep ourselves from falling. It is the Lord that does so.

"My sheep hear My voice, and I know them, and they follow Me: And I *give* unto them *eternal life;* and they *shall never perish, neither shall any man pluck them out of My hand.* My Father, which gave them Me, is greater than all; and *no man is able to pluck them out of My Father's hand*" (John 10:27-29).

"and I give unto them eternal life, and they *shall never get lost, and no one shall snatch them out of My hand*" (John 10:28 Williams).

"And I give them eternal life, and they *shall never lose it or perish throughout the ages — to all eternity they shall never by any means be destroyed. And no one is able to snatch them out of My hand*" (John 10:28 Amplified Bible).

The word "man" is not in the Greek text in either the 28th or 29th verse. It should be translated   "no one" or "none." This means that "no one" can take one, who has been saved, out of Christ's hand or out of the Father's hand — not a man, not an angel, not Satan, *not even the "saved one" himself!*

Notice in these verses that:

> The life is *given;*
>
> Its length is *eternal;*
>
> Those given it *shall never perish;*
>
> *None* can take them out of *Christ's hand;*
>
> *None* can take them out of the *Father's hand.*

If these verses are true (and they are!) we are eternally secure.

"When Jesus says, 'My sheep shall never perish,' it is unconditional and final. It is to be accepted in simple faith and made the subject of rejoicing and thanksgiving."[36]

11

DEAD TO THE LAW

God cannot overlook sin. "His name is *Love*, but He is as just as He is merciful, as true as He is gracious, and thus 'can by no means clear the guilty.' He can overlook nothing."[37] But Jesus, God's own Son, came and "put away sin by the sacrifice of Himself" (Hebrews 9:26). The penalty for our sin demanded by the law has been fully paid by Christ and will not be demanded again. *We are dead to the law,* because we are "in Christ." If we have accepted Christ as our Saviour, *the law can no longer condemn us.* We are eternally saved.

"Wherefore, my brethren, *ye also are become dead to the law by the body of Christ;* that ye should be married to another, even to Him who is raised from the dead, that we should bring forth fruit unto God" (Romans 7:4).

"Likewise, my brethren, *you have undergone death as to the Law through the* [*crucified*] *body of Christ,* so that now you may belong to Another, to Him who was raised from the dead in order that we may bear fruit for God" (Romans 7:4 Amplified Bible).

The penalty demanded by the law has been fully paid by my substitute, Jesus Christ. Therefore the law has no more power over me. The penalty demanded by the law for my sins will never be demanded of me. I am dead to the law and so is every born-again believer.

"For I through the law am dead to the law, that I might live unto God" (Galatians 2:19).

"For I through the Law — under the operation [of the curse] of the Law — have [in Christ's death for me] myself died to the Law and all the Law's demands upon me, so that I may [henceforth] live to and for God" (Galatians 2:19 Amplified Bible).

"Thus the death sentence has not only been imposed; the sinner who believes in Christ, has in the Person of Christ been executed and from thenceforth he cannot be condemned by the law for he is dead in its sight. Thus one who has been saved by being ransomed by the death of Christ cannot be lost."[38]

"What a tremendous statement! Paul does not say the law is dead. Far from it; but he says, 'I am dead to the law.' He is speaking of God's Holy, inviolable law, written upon the tables of stone; and says as far as that law is concerned, I am dead. In the eyes of the law, I don't even exist any more. The law does not even recognize my existence. So little power, so little application has that law to me. Let me repeat, therefore, Paul does not say, 'The law is dead.' It is very, very much alive. It still curses, it still condemns the sinner, it still is the ministration of death. It still demands the death of the transgressor. But, says Paul, as far as I am concerned, the law cannot touch me any more. I am beyond its reach forever, for 'I through the law am dead to the law.' "[39]

"For the law of the Spirit of life in Christ Jesus hath made me *free from the law of sin and death.* For what the law could not do, in that it was weak through the flesh, God sending His own Son in the likeness of sinful flesh, and for sin, condemned sin in the flesh" (Romans 8:2-3).

I am "free from the law of sin and death." Therefore it can no longer condemn me.

"All we like sheep have gone astray; we have turned every one to his own way; and *the LORD hath laid on Him the iniquity of us all*" (Isaiah 53:6).

My sins were put on *Christ.*

"For Christ also hath once suffered for sins, the just for the unjust, that He might bring us to God, *being put to death* in the flesh, but quickened by the Spirit" (1 Peter 3:18).

God judged Christ for my sin instead of me. His death was counted as my death. The penalty of the law has been carried out.

> "Who His own self bare our sins in His own body on the tree, that we, being *dead to sins,* should live unto righteousness: by whose stripes ye were healed" (1 Peter 2:24).

Christ took the penalty for *my* sin.

> "Christ hath redeemed us from the curse of the law, being made a curse for us: for it is written, Cursed is every one that hangeth on a tree" (Galatians 3:13).

Christ Himself took the curse of the law *for us.* The law has been fulfilled. We, who believe, are free from its curse.

> "But when the fulness of the time was come, God sent forth His Son, made of a woman, made under the law, *To redeem them that were under the law,* that we might receive the adoption of sons" (Galatians 4:4-5).

> *"If one who is saved is to be lost, it is necessary to return him into the state of being under the law. As he was freed from the law by payment of the death penalty, he can be brought back under it only by undoing the execution of his substitute. Until that is done, the law can have nothing to say to him."* [40]

"Suppose a man has committed a terrible crime, let us say the crime of murder. He has deserved the penalty of the law which is life imprisonment or death. He is therefore arrested and brought into court before the judge. The witnesses are called, one by one, and all testify with one accord to the man's guilt. There seems to be no defense for him at all. He is guilty and according to the law should be put to death. But, before sentence is pronounced upon the man, or the trial is over, something suddenly happens to him. While he is on the stand during the trial, the man suddenly grasps his throat, his face becomes blue, his eyes bulge out, he stiffens in every muscle and then suddenly slumps down in his chair and passes out. The physician is called, and pronounces the criminal dead.

"Now what does the judge do? Does he continue the trial?

Does he hear the rest of the testimonies? Of course not. The law cannot try a dead man. It applies only to living men. The man is dead. He is beyond the reach of the law, and so the judge raps his gavel and solemnly announces the case dismissed and the court adjourned. The man is dead in the eyes of the law.''[41]

The Apostle Paul was also "dead to the law," dead as far as the law was concerned, and so is every born-again believer. The penalty of the law has already been carried out against him in the person of God's Son, Jesus. The law can no longer condemn him. He is secure forever.

12

SIN NOT CHARGED AGAINST US

Since our sin has been charged to Christ and He has paid its penalty and we have accepted Him as our Saviour, it will not be charged against us. If our sins are "forgiven," "covered," "not imputed" to us, remembered "no more," then on what grounds can we be lost?

> "Saying, Blessed are they whose *iquities are forgiven,* and whose *sins are covered.* Blessed is the man to whom the Lord *will not impute sin"* (Romans 4:7-8).

Our sin has already been charged to Christ. If we accept His payment for our sin it will never be charged to us. The Lord "will not impute sin" to us; He has forgiven us all our trespasses; He will remember our sins and iniquities no more. Can such a one be lost?

> "To wit, that God was in Christ, reconciling the world unto Himself, *not imputing their trespasses unto them;* and hath committed unto us the word of reconciliation" (2 Corinthians 5:19).

> "namely, that God was in Christ reconciling the world to Himself, *not counting their trespasses against them,* and He has committed to us the word of reconciliation" (2 Corinthians 5:19 New American Standard).

> "And you, being dead in your sins and the uncircumcision of your flesh, hath He quickened together with Him, having forgiven you all trespasses" (Colossians 2:13).

>"And *their sins and iniquities will I remember no more.* Now where remission of these is, there is no more offering for sin" (Hebrews 10:17-18).

>" '*I will never, never any more recall their sins and deeds of wrong.*' But when these are forgiven, there is no more need of an offering for sin" (Hebrews 10:17-18 Williams).

"How utterly wonderful are these words! The infinite holy God, who knows all about all human sins and iniquities, who alone saith of man, 'I know their thoughts,' declares to His saints, I will remember (your) sins and iniquities no more. Surely *all* things are possible with God!"[42]

"Would it might sink into the heart of every reader that the only offering for sin that will ever be made *has* been made on the Cross, and can be rested in by any willing heart! ... The soul that leans or rests on that *one offering* will spend eternity in the delights of Heaven!"[43]

13

CHASTENING

"Chastening" is corrective judgment. It is punishment with the object of purifying the life. It may be translated "child training."[44] God chastens His own in love when they disobey and sin. He does not condemn them to be lost, for the penalty for their sin has already been paid by Christ. He chastens them *now,* in this life, to correct them and bring them into line with His will. Sin that is known and cherished in the life of a Christian causes broken fellowship with God and will bring chastening but not the loss of salvation.

> "And ye have forgotten the exhortation which speaketh unto you as unto children, My son, despise not thou the chastening of the Lord, nor faint when thou art rebuked of Him: For whom the Lord loveth He chasteneth, and scourgeth every son whom He receiveth. If ye endure chastening, God dealeth with you as with sons; for what son is he whom the father chasteneth not? But if ye be without chastisement, whereof all are partakers, then are ye bastards, and not sons. Furthermore we have had fathers of our flesh which corrected us, and we gave them reverence: shall we not much rather be in subjection unto the Father of spirits, and live? For they verily for a few days chastened us after their own pleasure; but He for our profit, that we might be partakers of His holiness. Now no chastening for the present seemeth to be joyous, but grievous: nevertheless afterward it yieldeth the peaceable fruit of righteousness unto them which are exercised thereby" (Hebrews 12:5-11).

God deals with us "as with sons." "Chastening is a provision of God exclusively for those who are sons; that is, saved. *It is for no others and no son is excluded* (Hebrews 12:6-8)."[45]

He chastens us because He loves us. The "world" is under the wrath of God and therefore under His condemnation. This is not true of the child of God, for he is an object of God's love. If God, then, in love, has made a special provision for His children, who persist in sinning, to keep them from being lost (chastening) (1 Corinthians 11:32), how can they be lost? [46]

"My friend, if you claim to be a Christian and there is no trial for you to face, no testings for you to go through, you may well look to it; this passage tells us that all of God's sons are partakers of chastening. As a matter of fact, chastening is the badge of our legitimacy."[47]

> "For he that eateth and drinketh unworthily, eateth and drinketh damnation to himself, not discerning the Lord's body. For this cause many are weak and sickly among you, and many sleep" (1 Corinthians 11:29-30).
>
> "For he who eats and drinks, eats and drinks judgment to himself, if he does not judge the body rightly. For this reason many among you are weak and sick, and a number sleep" (1 Corinthians 11:29-30 New American Standard).
>
> "For the one who eats and drinks is eating and drinking so as to bring judgment upon himself if he does not properly evaluate the body. Because of this, among you are many who have infirmities and are in continued ill health, and a considerable number are sleeping [dead]" (1 Corinthians 11:29-30 Wuest).

This passage is concerning Christians who were disorderly at the Lord's table. They ate and drank "judgment" or "chastening" to themselves. The word "damnation" is a poor translation. The result of the "judgment" is that many are "weak and sickly" and many "sleep." Sickness is one way in which God chastens. Some at Corinth are said to "sleep." The word "sleep" is used of the death of one who is saved (Matthew 27:52; John 11:11,13; Acts 7:60; 1 Corinthians 15:6,18,20,51; 1 Thessalonians 4:14). Their sin had been so serious that God had called them home to Himself so that they did not hinder His work on earth, but they are not lost. The death of one who is lost is not called "sleep."

"For if we would judge ourselves, we should not be judged. But when we are judged, *we are chastened of the Lord, that we should not be condemned with the world*" (1 Corinthians 11:31-32).

14

GOD'S FOREKNOWLEDGE AND ELECTION

God's knowledge is perfect. He is omniscient — that is to say, He knows *everything*, not only things in the past and present but in the future as well. He knows everything that has happened, that is happening, and that will happen. God knew my failures and weaknesses before He ever saved me. To say that one whom God foreknew and saved could be lost would be to say that God made a mistake, either because His foreknowledge of him was not correct or because He saved him by mistake, since He knew ahead of time that he would be lost.

> "Remember the former things of old: for I am God, and there is none else; I am God, and there is none like Me, *Declaring the end from the beginning, and from ancient times the things that are not yet done,* saying, My counsel shall stand, and I will do all My pleasure" (Isaiah 46:9-10).

God knows everything ahead of time. When God declares that certain things will happen — they will happen. God knows all about you and me. In fact, He knew everything that we would do before we were ever born.

> "Known unto God are all His works from the beginning of the world" (Acts 15:18).

"From an eternity past He knew every detail which would ever come to pass into the eternity of the future. Otherwise, how else could He plan anything? God must be omniscient and know all things, or cease to be a sovereign God. He must be omniscient or we cannot trust Him, for then He might be surprised by the events which He did not foreknow and foresee, and thus become a being of chance and not one of destiny."[48]

> "Thine eyes did see my substance, yet being unperfect; and in Thy book all my members were written, which in continuance were fashioned, when as yet there was none of them" (Psalm 139:16).

> "But Jesus did not commit Himself unto them, *because He knew all men*, And needed not that any should testify of man: for He knew what was in man" (John 2:24-25).

> "*Elect according to the foreknowledge of God the father,* through sanctification of the Spirit, unto obedience and sprinkling of the blood of Jesus Christ: Grace unto you, and peace, be multiplied" (1 Peter 1:2).

> "Chosen in accordance with the foreknowledge of God"(1 Peter 1:2a Williams).

God knew all about our entire lives when He "chose" (elected) *us.*

> "*According as He hath chosen us in Him before the foundation of the world,* that we should be holy and without blame before Him in love" (Ephesians 1:4).

God chose us *"before the foundation of the world"* even though He already knew all of our failures and weaknesses, even though He already knew all of our sins. Did He make a mistake? If a saved one can be lost, He did. M. R. DeHaan writes: "If He knew that you would...ultimately be lost, then why would He choose you in the first place? Why choose you at all? Why save you in the first place, if He knew it would not last?"[49]

> "For *whom He did foreknow,* He also did predestinate to be conformed to the image of His Son, that He might be the firstborn among many brethren. Moreover whom He did predestinate, them He also called: and whom He called, them He also justified: and whom He justified, them He also glorified" (Romans 8:29-30).

God *knew us* before we were ever born. Not just our deeds; He knew *us.* We are *foreknown, predestinated, called, justified, glorified.*

All of this list is true of all believers. *"Just as many are glorified as are predestinated. Not a single one less."*[50] All of this is stated as already accomplished. *We are already glorified.* Only the manifestation of our glorification is still future. It is as sure as was the manifestation of Christ, who was "foreordained before the foundation of the world, but was manifest in these last times for you" (1 Peter 1:20) Our appearance in glory is yet future (Colossians 3:3-4), but our glorification has already been accomplished!

Newell says, "This is the necessary end of this amazing series — *glorified!* Thus must these foreknown ones be ever, before God, since God foreknew them in Christ. None has yet been glorified in manifestation. Indeed, Christ Himself has not yet been 'manifested'; although He has entered into His glory. And it is in this glorified Christ that God chose us long ago, before the foundation of the world! God, who could thus connect us to Christ, can also say of us, I have glorified them! And so the saints go on to a glory already true of them by the word of their God!"[51]

Also notice that all who are "foreknown" (that is, all believers) are also "predestinated." They are predestinated "to be conformed to the image of His Son." If God has determined before the foundation of the world that my destiny is to be conformed to the image of His Son, then, how can I have any other destiny? How can I be lost?

> *"Who shall lay any thing to the charge of God's elect?* It is God that justifieth. Who is he that condemneth? It is Christ that died, yea rather, that is risen again, who also maketh intercession for us" (Romans 8:33-34).

> "Who can bring any charge against those whom God has chosen? It is God who declared them in right standing; who can condemn them?" (Romans 8:33 Williams)

> "Who shall bring any charge against God's elect [when it is] God who justifies— who puts us in right relation to Himself? (Who shall come forward and accuse or impeach those whom God has chosen? Will God, who acquits us?)" (Romans 8:33 Amplified Bible)

God has declared us righteous, and that before the foundation of the world (Ephesians 1:4), and that even though He knew us and all about us (1 Peter 1:2; Romans 8:29). Certainly no one can condemn us! "Shall any stand before God's high court and condemn *whom He has justified?* Never!"[52]

"Will God who has redeemed us and purchased us and declared us 'justified,' find fault with or repudiate His own work? Perish the thought!"[53]

> "Who hath saved us, and called us with an holy calling, not according to our works, but according to His own purpose and grace, *which was given us in Christ Jesus before the world began*" (2 Timothy 1:9).

> "which He gave us in Christ Jesus before the beginning of time" (2 Timothy 1:9b Montgomery).

> "which was shown us through union with Christ Jesus eternal ages ago" (2 Timothy 1:9b Williams).

Notice the time here. We who are saved were *"in Christ"* — *"in union with Christ"* before the world began. Only the manifestation of this already accomplished fact awaits the appearance of Christ (2 Timothy 1:10).

> "And that He might make known the riches of His glory on the vessels of mercy, *which He had afore prepared unto glory.* Even us, whom He hath called, not of the Jews only, but also of the Gentiles?" (Romans 9:23-24)

"Mark well here this word 'afore.' For the whole process of our salvation is viewed from that blessed future day when we shall enter, through divine mercy, into that glory unto which God 'afore' appointed us, and for which He 'afore' prepared us, in the work of Christ for us, and the application to us of that work, by the blessed Holy Spirit. All was 'afore' arranged by God!"[54]

If we are "afore prepared unto glory" by God and we could lose our salvation then God made a mistake in His preparation of us.

> "But we are bound to give thanks alway to God for you, brethren beloved of the Lord, because God hath *from the beginning chosen you* to salvation through sanctification of the Spirit, and belief of

the truth" (2 Thessalonians 2:13).

> "*Before I formed thee in the belly I knew thee;* and *before thou camest forth out of the womb I sanctified thee,* and I ordained thee a prophet unto the nations" (Jeremiah 1:5).

Here is a clear example of God's foreknowledge and His choosing of a man for a particular task before that man was even conceived. God knew Jeremiah before Jeremiah ever existed. The same God who knew Jeremiah also knew us before the foundation of the world and in accordance with that foreknowledge, chose us (1 Peter 1:2; Ephesians 1:4; Romans 8:33-34; 2 Timothy 1:9; 2 Thessalonians 2:13). It is inconceivable that such a one could be lost!

> "And all that dwell upon the earth shall worship him, whose names are not written in the book of life of the Lamb slain from the foundation of the world" (Revelation 13:8).

> "And all who dwell on the earth will worship him, every one whose name has not been written from the foundation of the world in the book of life of the Lamb who has been slain" (Revelation 13:8 New American Standard).

> "All the inhabitants of the earth whose names, from the foundation of the world, have not been written in the slaughtered Lamb's book of life, will worship him" (Revelation 13:8 Williams).

> "The beast that thou sawest was, and is not; and shall ascend out of the bottomless pit, and go into perdition: and they that dwell on the earth shall wonder, whose names were not written in the book of life from the foundation of the world, when they behold the beast that was, and is not, and yet is" (Revelation 17:8).

> "The Wild Beast whom you saw was, and is not, and is destined to be ascending out of the bottomless place, and he goes off into perdition. And those who dwell on the earth shall wonder, whose names have not been permanently inscribed upon the scroll of life from the time of the foundation of the universe, when they see the Wild Beast, how that he was and is not and shall come" (Revelation 17:8 Wuest).

The "book of life" is mentioned in the following verses: Philippians 4:3; Revelation 3:5; 13:8; 20:12,15; 21:27. From Revelation 20:12, 15 we learn that everyone whose name is not in the "book of life" will be cast into the "lake of fire." From Revelation 21:27 we learn that only those whose names are written in the "book of life" will be allowed to enter "New Jerusalem." In the verses quoted above (Revelation 13:8 together with 17:8) we see that those whose names were not written in the "book of life *from the foundation of the world"* will follow and worship the "beast" (the wicked world ruler to come). If a person's name is in the "book of life," then it must have been put there *before the "foundation of the world."*

The word translated "written" in Revelation 13:8 and 17:8 is a tense in the Greek which signifies an action completed in time past with results continuing into the present. It means that there are those whose names were not written in the "book of life" before the foundation of the world and as a continuing result are not written there now.

God chose (elected) us, who are saved, according to His foreknowledge (1 Peter 1:2). He chose us *before the foundation of the world* (Ephesians 1:4). The names of those chosen were evidently written in the "book of life" then (before the foundation of the world) and they have been there ever since.

In Revelation 3:5 God promises that He will not blot out of the "book of life" the name of "he that overcometh" (that is, *every born-again believer,* 1 John 5:4-5).

If God knew *all* about me before the foundation of the world (and He did) and He chose me anyway and wrote my name in the "book of life" (and He did), and He has promised not to blot it out (and He has), then *there is no possible way for me to be lost!*

(Note: The phrase in Revelation 22:19 translated in the King James Version "book of life" would be better translated "tree of life." The word in the Greek is not the word for book but is the same word translated "tree" in Revelation 22:2. It is translated "tree of life" by most newer translations — Williams, Wuest, New American Standard, Amplified, etc.)

15

INDWELT AND SEALED BY THE HOLY SPIRIT

The Bible teaches that every born-again Christian is "indwelt" by the Holy Spirit (Romans 8:9), that our bodies are the "temple" of the Holy Spirit (1 Corinthians 6:19), that He will abide with us forever (John 14:16), that we are "sealed" with the Holy Spirit "unto the day of redemption." For one "indwelt" and "sealed" by the Holy Spirit to be lost would mean that the Holy Spirit would have to be withdrawn and the "seal" broken, but God says that the Spirit will dwell with us "forever" and the "seal" is "unto the day of redemption."

> "In whom ye also trusted, after that ye heard the word of truth, the gospel of your salvation: in whom also after that ye believed, *ye were sealed with that holy Spirit* of promise, Which is the *earnest* of our inheritance until the redemption of the *purchased possession*, unto the praise of His glory" (Ephesians 1:13-14).

> "Who hath also *sealed us,* and *given the earnest of the Spirit* in our hearts" (2 Corinthians 1:22).

"A seal was a stamp, a mark of ownership, a mark of approval.... God the Father seals us by the Spirit, and says, as it were, 'This man, this woman, belongs to Me; henceforth I stand back of him, I own him as Mine.' "[55]

We are sealed with the Holy Spirit "until the redemption of the purchased possession." Lehman Strauss writes, "We are not sealed *by* the Spirit but, rather, *with* the Spirit. Better still, the Spirit is the seal."[56] Lewis Sperry Chafer writes, "The Spirit Himself is the seal. His blessed presence in every true child of God is the divine mark of ownership, purpose, and destiny. The

Spirit who was sent to abide in us will not withdraw. He may be grieved, or quenched (resisted), but He abides. This He does as the divine guaranty that there shall be no failure in any purpose of God and the sealed one will reach his eternal glory and the blessedness of 'the day of redemption.' "[57]

Christ has paid the price of our redemption. He has purchased us with His own blood at the cross, We are His, and the "seal" of the Holy Spirit is proof of the transaction.

Notice also that the Holy Spirit is the "earnest" of the believer's inheritance. "Earnest money is a payment made by a purchaser to guarantee the completion of the transaction by him. In Christ, the believer has obtained an inheritance which was 'predestinated according to the purpose of Him who worketh all things after the counsel of His own will' (Ephesians 1:11).

"The believer has not yet entered into possession of this inheritance, but the Holy Spirit has been given as an earnest that it shall be given when the transaction has been fully consummated. To say that one who has been saved can be lost is to say that possession of the inheritance shall not be given to one to whom God has already made an earnest payment. 'God is not a man, that He should lie; neither the son of man, that He should repent: hath He said, and shall He not do it? or hath He spoken, and shall He not make it good?' (Numbers 23:19)."[58]

The phrase "Which is the earnest of our inheritance" is translated:

"Who is the first installment of our inheritance" (Williams)

"Who is given as a pledge of our inheritance" (New American Standard)

"That [Spirit] is the guarantee of our inheritance — the first fruit, the pledge and foretaste, the down payment on our heritage." (Amplified Bible)

> "And grieve not the holy Spirit of God, whereby *ye are sealed unto the day of redemption*" (Ephesians 4:30).

"The point of greatest significance in the sealing of the Holy Spirit is the eternal security of the believer. It is plainly stated that the seal is placed on the Christian with a view to keeping him

safe unto the day of redemption — the time of complete
deliverance from all sin. The matter is not left in human hands,
but is dependent entirely on the power of God. The nature of the
seal forbids any possibility of counterfeit or disallowing of the
token. The person of the Holy Spirit, possessing all the attributes
of God, by His presence is a token of God's abiding grace which
could not be excelled. As God has promised that His Spirit will
abide in the believer, so the Spirit Himself as the seal of our
salvation brings all assurance to the believer's heart."[59]

> "But *ye are not in the flesh, but in the Spirit,* if so be that the
> Spirit of God dwell in you. Now *if any man have not the Spirit of
> Christ, he is none of His.* And if Christ be in you, the body is dead
> because of sin; but the Spirit is life because of righteousness. But if
> the *Spirit* of Him that raised up Jesus from the dead dwell in you,
> He that raised up Christ from the dead *shall also* quicken your
> mortal bodies by His Spirit that dwelleth in you" (Romans 8:9-
> 11).

All born-again believers have the Spirit dwelling within
them. We have already been "quickened" (made alive)
spiritually (Ephesians 2:1,5). "The Spirit of God dwells in none
but those whom He has quickened. And He *dwells* in all whom He
has quickened."[60]

All who have the Spirit (and this is all born-again believers —
verse 9) shall also have their mortal bodies quickened (made
alive). "This mortal must put on immortality" (1 Corinthians
15:53). There is no question about this being done. If you have
been "quickened" spiritually you will also have your mortal body
"quickened."

> "And I will pray the Father, and He shall give you another
> Comforter, *that He may abide with you for ever;* Even the Spirit of
> truth; whom the world cannot receive, because it seeth Him not,
> neither knoweth Him: but ye know Him; for *He dwelleth with you,
> and shall be in you"* (John 14:16-17).

Does Jesus here promise that the "Comforter" (the Holy
Spirit) will abide with them until they become lost? No! He
promises that He will "abide with you *for ever."* Was He wrong?

> "What? know ye not that *your body is the temple of the Holy*

Ghost which is in you, which ye have of God, and *ye are not your own?*" (1 Corinthians 6:19)

The Holy Spirit *is* in us. We are not our own. Can we take ourselves away from our owner?

"But the anointing which ye have received of Him abideth in you, and ye need not that any man teach you: but as the same anointing teacheth you of all things, and is truth, and is no lie, and even as it hath taught you, ye shall abide in Him" (1 John 2:27).

The "anointing" is the Holy Spirit and He abides (remains) in us.

16

OUR ADVOCATE AND INTERCESSOR

Satan, the "accuser of the brethren," is always accusing us before God, pointing out our sin to Him. Christ, however, is our "advocate," our "intercessor," who pleads our case for us. He points out that the sins, of which Satan accuses us, have already been paid for at Calvary by the blood of Himself. With Christ Himself as our advocate it is not possible for us to be lost!

"Who is he that condemneth? It is Christ that died, yea rather, that is risen again, who is even at the right hand of God, who also *maketh intercession for us*" (Romans 8:34).

"Wherefore He is able also to save them to the uttermost that come unto God by Him, seeing He *ever liveth to make intercession for them*" (Hebrews 7:25).

"My little children, these things write I unto you, that ye sin not. And if any man sin, we have an *advocate* with the Father, Jesus Christ the righteous" (1 John 2:1).

If sin in the life of a believer will cause him to be condemned, then for what purpose is there an "intercessor" or "advocate"?

Christ is our intercessor or advocate because Christians do sin and because the "accuser of the brethren" (Satan — Revelation 12:10) is accusing us before God day and night, we need an advocate, an intercessor. Christ is that advocate and pleads for us, not on the ground that we will do better if God does not judge us, but on the ground of His shed blood at Calvary, where He paid for our sin once and for all; on the ground that the penalty for sin has been paid and cannot be demanded a second time.

> "*Much more* then, being now justified by His blood, *we shall be saved from wrath through Him.* For if, when we were enemies, we were reconciled to God by the death of His Son, *much more,* being reconciled, *we shall be saved by His life*" (Romans 5:9-10).

Since we have already been reconciled to God by the death of His Son, these verses say that it is *much more* certain that we shall be saved by His life! (That is His intercession — for "He ever liveth to make intercession" — Hebrews 7:25).

Our salvation is then secure because Christ is interceding for us. "He is able to save — to the uttermost," to the completion, to the end!

17

OUR UNION WITH CHRIST

When a believer truly sees his standing "in Christ," his union with Christ, there ceases to be any question concerning his security. The believer is "in Christ" and Christ is in him. He is a member of Christ's body. "In Christ" the believer's sin is counted as Christ's sin and at the cross He (Christ) paid its penalty. "In Christ," Christ's death, burial, and resurrection are counted as the believer's death, burial, and resurrection. "In Christ" the believer is declared righteous. He does not stand in his righteousness but in the righteousness of Christ. The believer's present standing before God and his eternal future is inseparably linked with that of Christ. *"In Christ" the believer is as secure for eternity as is Christ Himself.*

OUR UNION WITH CHRIST — "IN CHRIST"

Throughout the New Testament believers are repeatedly said to be "in Christ" or "in Him." The Bible says that we are "baptized" into (immersed into or placed into) the body of Christ. "To be in Christ is to possess a new standing before God; a standing which is no less than the infinite righteousness of God."[61]

"For by one Spirit are we all baptized into one body, whether we be Jews or Gentiles, whether we be bond or free; and have been all made to drink into one Spirit" (1 Corinthians 12:13).

"for indeed by means of one Spirit we all were *placed into one body*, whether Jews or Gentiles, whether slaves or free men. And we all were imbued with one Spirit" (1 Corinthians 12:13 Wuest).

The moment that we believed we were placed by the Holy Spirit into the "body of Christ." (Read the entire context of this passage — 1 Corinthians 12:12-31.)

"Know ye not, that so many of us as were baptized into Jesus Christ were baptized into His death?" (Romans 6:3)

"Do you not know that all we who were *placed in Christ Jesus*, in His death were placed?" (Romans 6:3 Wuest)

"For as many of you as have been baptized into Christ have put on Christ. There is neither Jew nor Greek, there is neither bond nor free, there is neither male nor female: for ye are all one in Christ Jesus" (Galatians 3:27-28).

"for as many as were introduced *into union with Christ*, put on Christ. There is neither Jew nor Greek, there is neither slave nor free, there is neither male nor female. For you are all one in Christ Jesus" (Galatians 3:27-28 Wuest).

"Now ye are the *body of Christ*, and *members in particular*" (1 Corinthians 12:27).

Here we see our union with Christ. If He is safe then we are safe. A. J. Gordon writes, "And will Christ permit this body to be dismembered? He can suffer in His members (Acts 22:7); but Faith would feel herself robbed of all her heritage of assurance, were it anywhere written, He can be cut off or perish in His members. Wounds and mutilations there will be; for, in Rutherford's strong phrase, 'The Dragon will strike at Christ so long as there is one bit or portion of His mystical body out of heaven.' But love cannot cherish the fear that He will heal the hurts of His people slightly, much less sunder them from Him by an external excision. For 'no man ever yet hated his own [body]; but *nourisheth* and *cherisheth* it, even as the Lord the church: For we are members of His body, of His flesh, and of His bones!' " [62]

"For we are *members of His body, of His flesh, and of His bones*" (Ephesians 5:30).

We are "members of His body." Our destiny is linked with His destiny. Where He is for eternity, there will we be also (John 14:3).

> "Therefore if any man be *in Christ,* he is a new creature: old things are passed away; behold, all things are become new" (2 Corinthians 5:17).

> "Therefore if any person is (*ingrafted*) *in Christ,* the Messiah, he is (a new creature altogether,) a new creation; the old (previous moral and spiritual condition) has passed away. Behold, the fresh and new has come!" (2 Corinthians 5:17 Amplified Bible)

> "So if anybody is *in union with Christ,* he is the work of a new creation; the old condition has passed away, a new condition has come" (2 Corinthians 5:17 Williams).

Every born-again believer is "in Christ." For the believer to be lost, his union with Christ would have to cease. He would have to be taken out of Christ. On what grounds could he be taken out? He did not receive his standing "in Christ" because of any merit of his own so he cannot lose it by demerit or lack of merit. Where in God's Word is one "in Christ" ever said to be taken out of Christ?

> "For we are His workmanship, created *in Christ Jesus* unto good works, which God hath before ordained that we should walk in them" (Ephesians 2:10).

> "For He has made us what we are, because He has created us through our *union with Christ Jesus* for doing good deeds which He beforehand planned for us to do" (Ephesians 2:10 Williams).

We are in union with Christ. It is as a result of this union that our good works come.

> "There is therefore now no condemnation to them which are *in Christ Jesus*" (Romans 8:1).

For those who are "in Christ" there is "no condemnation." Since Christ cannot be condemned eternally, neither can we, for we are "in Him" (The last part of Romans 8:1 is not quoted since it is not in the better manuscripts.)

"Paul, an apostle of Jesus Christ by the will of God, to the saints which are at Ephesus, and to the faithful *in Christ Jesus*" (Ephesians 1:1).

"Paul, by God's will an apostle of Christ Jesus, to God's people who are faithful *in Christ Jesus*" (Ephesians 1:1 Williams).

"Blessed be the God and Father of our Lord Jesus Christ, who hath blessed us with all spiritual blessings in heavenly places *in Christ*" (Ephesians 1:3).

It is because of our *union with Christ,* because we are *"in Him,"* that we have "all spiritual blessings."

"According as He hath chosen us *in Him* before the foundation of the world, that we should be holy and without blame before Him in love" (Ephesians 1:4).

"Even as [in His love] He chose us — actually picked us out for Himself as His own — *in Christ* before the foundation of the world; that we should be holy (consecrated and set apart for Him) and blameless in His sight, even above reproach, before Him in love" (Ephesians 1:4 Amplified Bible).

We were chosen "in Christ" before the foundation of the world. If our union with Christ was decided by God before the foundation of the world then for us to lose that position would mean that God's choice of us would have to be overthrown.

"*In whom* we have redemption through His blood, the forgiveness of sins, according to the riches of His grace" (Ephesians 1:7).

"*It is through union with Him* that we have redemption by His blood and the forgiveness of our shortcomings, in accordance with the generosity of His unmerited favor which He lavished upon us" (Ephesians 1:7 Williams).

"*In whom* also we have obtained an inheritance, being predestinated according to the purpose of Him who worketh all things after the counsel of His own will" (Ephesians 1:11).

"But now *in Christ Jesus* ye who sometimes were far off are made nigh by the blood of Christ" (Ephesians 2:13).

"But of Him are ye *in Christ Jesus,* who of God is made unto us

wisdom, and righteousness, and sanctification, and redemption"
(1 Corinthians 1:30).

"And ye are complete *in Him,* which is the head of all prin-
cipality and power: *In whom* also ye are circumcised with the
circumcision made without hands, in putting off the body of the
sins of the flesh by the circumcision of Christ" (Colossians 2:10-
11).

See also Romans 6:3-8; 8:2,39; 12:4-5; 16:7,10; 1 Corinthians 1:2; 3:1; 4:10,15,17; 6:15; 8:6; 12:13-31; 15:18,19,22,58;
2 Corinthians 1:21; 2:14,17; 3:13-14; 5:21; 12:2; Galatians
1:22; 2:4; 5:6; 6:15; Ephesians 1:10,13,22-23; 2:5-6,20,22;
3:12; 6:10; Philippians 1:1,13,21,26; 3:3,9,14; 4:21; Colossians
1:2,4,14,28; 2:3,6-7,9,12; 3:3-4; 1 Thessalonians 1:1,3; 2:14;
4:14,16; 5:18; 2 Thessalonians 1:1,12; 1 Timothy 1:14; 2
Timothy 1:9; 2:1; 3:12,15; Philemon 6,8,20,23; 1 Peter 1:8;
5:14; 1 John 2:6; Jude 1.

OUR UNION WITH CHRIST — CHRIST IN US

Not only are believers said to be "in Christ" but Christ is in
believers. A. J. Gordon writes: "The union of the believer with
his Lord is a *reciprocal* union. 'Ye in Me, and I in you.' Through it
Christ both gives and takes, gives the Father's life and
blessedness, and takes the believer's death and wretchedness.
'All that Christ has,' says Luther, 'now becomes the property of
the believing soul; all that the soul has becomes the property
of Christ. Christ possesses every blessing and eternal salvation;
they are henceforth the property of the soul. The soul possesses
every vice and sin; they become henceforth the property of
Christ.' "[63]

"I am crucified with Christ: nevertheless I live; yet not I, but
Christ liveth in me: and the life which I now live in the flesh I live
by the faith of the Son of God, who loved me, and gave Himself for
me" (Galatians 2:20).

"I have been crucified with Christ — [in Him] I have shared His
crucifixion; it is no longer I who live, but *Christ,* the Messiah, *lives*

in me; and the life I now live in the body I live by faith — by adherence to and reliance on and [complete] trust — in the Son of God, Who loved me and gave Himself up for me" (Galatians 2:20 Amplified Bible).

"For me *to live is Christ,* and to die is gain" (Philippians 1:21).

"For me, *to live is Christ — His life in me;* and to die is gain — [the gain of the glory of eternity]" (Philippians 1:21 Amplified Bible).

"And if *Christ be in you,* the body is dead because of sin; but the Spirit is life because of righteousness" (Romans 8:10).

"But if *Christ lives in you,* although your bodies must die because of sin, your spirits are now enjoying life because of right standing with God" (Romans 8:10 Williams).

"But if *Christ lives in you,* [then although your natural] body is dead by reason of sin and guilt, the spirit is alive because of [the] righteousness [that He imputes to you]" (Romans 8:10 Amplified Bible).

"To whom God would make known what is the riches of the glory of this mystery among the Gentiles; which is *Christ in you,* the hope of glory" (Colossians 1:27).

"*I in them,* and Thou in Me, that they may be made perfect in one; and that the world may know that Thou hast sent Me, and hast loved them, as Thou hast loved Me" (John 17:23).

"*I in union with them* and You in union with Me, so that they may be perfectly united, and the world may be sure that You sent Me and that You have loved them just as You have loved Me" (John 17:23 Williams).

Because we are "in Christ" and He is in us, God, the Father, loves us just as He loves Christ, His own Son!

OUR UNION WITH CHRIST —
OUR SIN COUNTED AS HIS

Because I am "in Christ" my sin is counted as Christ's, though He had no sin, and He died for my sin, paying its penalty for me.

"For He hath *made Him to be sin for us,* who knew no sin; that we might be made the righteousness of God in Him" (2 Corinthians 5:21).

Jesus, God's own sinless Son, was made "sin for us." Our sin was counted as His and He bore its penalty at Calvary.

"But *He was wounded for our transgressions, He was bruised for our iniquities: the chastisement of our peace was upon Him; and with His stripes we are healed.* All we like sheep have gone astray; we have turned every one to his own way; and the *LORD hath laid on Him the iniquity of us all"* (Isaiah 53:5-6).

He has borne our sin as if it were His own. Our sin (iniquity) was laid on Him. It was counted as His and He has taken its penalty.

"Therefore will I divide Him a portion with the great, and He shall divide the spoil with the strong; because He hath poured out His soul unto death: and He was numbered with the transgressors; *and He bare the sin of many,* and made intercession for the transgressors" (Isaiah 53:12).

"Who *His own self bare our sins in His own body* on the tree, that we, being dead to sins, should live unto righteousness: by whose stripes ye were healed" (1 Peter 2:24).

"*He personally bore our sins* in His [own] body to the tree [as to an altar and offered Himself on it], that we might die (cease to exist) to sin and live to righteousness. By His wounds you have been healed" (1 Peter 2:24 Amplified Bible).

"For *Christ also hath once suffered for sins, the just for the unjust,* that He might bring us to God, being put to death in the flesh, but quickened by the Spirit" (1 Peter 3:18).

"For *Christ Himself, once for all, died for our sins,* the Innocent for the guilty to bring us to God, being put to death in physical form but made alive in the Spirit" (1 Peter 3:18 Williams).

"For *Christ, the Messiah,* [*Himself*] *died for sins once for all,* the Righteous for the unrighteous — the Just for the unjust, the Innocent for the guilty — that He might bring us to God. In His human body He was put to death but He was made alive in the spirit" (1 Peter 3:18 Amplified Bible).

"And *He is the propitiation for our sins:* and not for ours only, but also for the sins of the whole world" (1 John 2:2).

"And *He is Himself the atoning sacrifice for our sins;* and not for ours alone, but also for the whole world" (1 John 2:2 Williams).

"Herein is love, not that we loved God, but that He loved us, and *sent His Son to be the propitiation for our sins"* (1 John 4:10).

"In this way is seen the true love, not that we loved God but that He loved us and *sent His Son to be the atoning sacrifice for our sins"* (1 John 4:10 Williams).

"I am the good shepherd: the *good shepherd giveth His life for the sheep....* As the Father knoweth Me, even so know I the Father: and *I lay down My life for the sheep"* (John 10:11,15).

"Who was delivered *for our offences,* and was raised again for our justification" (Romans 4:25).

"For when we were yet without strength, in due time *Christ died for the ungodly....* But God commendeth His love toward us, in that, while we were yet sinners, *Christ died for us"* (Romans 5:6,8).

"He that spared not His own Son, but *delivered Him up for us all,* how shall He not with Him also freely give us all things?" (Romans 8:32)

"For I delivered unto you first of all that which I also received, how that *Christ died for our sins* according to the scriptures" (1 Corinthians 15:3).

"Who *gave Himself for our sins,* that He might deliver us from this present evil world, according to the will of God and our Father" (Galatians 1:4).

"So Christ was once offered to *bear the sins of many;* and unto them that look for Him shall He appear the second time without sin unto salvation" (Hebrews 9:28).

See also 1 Corinthians 5:7; Galatians 2:20; 3:13; Ephesians 5:2; 1 Timothy 2:6; Hebrews 9:26; 10:10,12,14; 1 Peter 1:18-19; 4:1.

In all of these verses we see that our sin was counted as Christ's. It was charged to Him. He took the penalty for our sin at

Calvary. If we are "in Christ" the penalty for all our sin has already been paid. Since this is true, sin cannot cause us to lose our salvation.

OUR UNION WITH CHIRST —
CHRIST'S DEATH, BURIAL, AND RESURRECTION
COUNTED AS OURS

Because I am "in Christ" His death is counted as my death, His burial as my burial, and His resurrection as my resurrection. Today I stand on resurrection ground "in Christ."

> "*I am crucified with Christ:* nevertheless I live; yet not I, but Christ liveth in me: and the life which I now live in the flesh I live by the faith of the Son of God, who loved me, and gave Himself for me" (Galatians 2:20).

> "*I have been crucified with Christ* — [*in Him*] *I have shared His crucifixion;* it is no longer I who live, but Christ, the Messiah, lives in me; and the life I now live in the body I live by faith — by adherence to and reliance on and [complete] trust — in the Son of God, Who loved me and gave Himself up for me" (Galatians 2:20 Amplified Bible).

"How vivid a reflection of his own experience do we find in Luther's pithy comment on these words: 'I am crucified with Christ.' 'Paul speaketh not here of crucifying by imitation or example; but he speaketh of that high crucifying whereby sin, the devil, and death, are crucified in Christ and not in me. Here Christ Jesus doth all Himself alone. But believing in Christ, I am by faith crucified also with Christ; so that all these things are crucified and dead with me.' — *Commentary on Galatians.*" [64]

If I could lose my salvation, my crucifixion with Christ would have to be annulled.

> "Wherefore if ye be *dead with Christ* from the rudiments of the world, why, as though living in the world, are ye subject to ordinances" (Colossians 2:20).

> *"For ye are dead,* and your life is hid with Christ in God" (Colossians 3:3).

Christ's death is counted as my death. Therefore as far as the "law" is concerned I am dead.

> "It is a faithful saying: For if we be *dead with Him,* we shall also live with Him" (2 Timothy 2:11).

Every born-again Christian *is* dead with Christ (Christ's death is counted as his). Therefore every born-again Christian shall "live with Him."

> "But we see Jesus, who was made a little lower than the angels for the suffering of death, crowned with glory and honour; that He by the grace of God *should taste death for every man"* (Hebrews 2:9).

> "Knowing this, that our old man is *crucified with Him,* that the body of sin might be destroyed, that henceforth we should not serve sin. For *he that is dead is freed from sin. Now if we be dead with Christ,* we believe that *we shall also live with Him"* (Romans 6:6-8).

> "Wherefore, my brethren, ye also are become *dead to the law by the body of Christ;* that ye should be married to another, even to Him who is raised from the dead, that we should bring forth fruit unto God" (Romans 7:4).

> "For I through the law am *dead to the law,* that I might live unto God" (Galatians 2:19).

Since my sin was counted as Christ's and His death was counted as mine, as far as the law is concerned I am dead. Its penalty has already been carried out. I am "in Christ." I am free from the law. It can no longer condemn me.

> "Buried with Him in baptism, wherein also *ye are risen with Him* through the faith of the operation of God, who hath raised Him from the dead" (Colossians 2:12).

> *"having been entombed with Him* in the placing into [Christ by the Holy Spirit], in which act of placing into [Christ] *you were also raised with Him* through your faith in the effectual working energy

of the God who raised Him out from among the dead" (Colossians 2:12 Wuest).

"And you, being dead in your sins and the uncircumcision of your flesh, *hath He quickened together with Him,* having forgiven you all *trespasses"* (Colossians 2:13).

"Neither yield ye your members as instruments of unrighteousness unto sin: but yield yourselves unto God, as *those that are alive from the dead,* and your members as instruments of righteousness unto God" (Romans 6:13).

"If ye then be *risen with Christ,* seek those things which are above, where Christ sitteth on the right hand of God" (Colossians 3:1).

"But God, who is rich in mercy, for His great love wherewith He loved us, Even when we were dead in sins, hath *quickened us together with Christ,* [*by grace ye are saved;*] *And hath raised us up together,* and made us sit together in heavenly places in Christ Jesus" (Ephesians 2:4-6).

"But God, who is so rich in mercy on account of the great love He has for us, has made us, though dead because of our short- comings, *live again in fellowship with Christ —* it is by His un- merited favor that you have been saved. And He *raised us with Him and through union with Christ Jesus* He made us sit down with Him in the heavenly realm" (Ephesians 2:4-6 Williams).

M. R. DeHaan writes, "What a remarkable statement, and what a glorious truth! What a wonderful position is ours! How sad, how tragic, that many, many professing Christians not understanding the grace of God, but being misled by the teaching that they are still under the law of commandments, worry, struggle, work, and toil to keep saved, when if they only knew the truth of grace, they would realize that they are already in Heaven with Christ, seated in the heavenlies. How many are trying to get to Heaven finally, by hanging on, enduring to the end, ob- serving the legality of the law, and ordinances, and the sabbath days; when if they only knew the grace of God, they could stop working to keep saved, and really start working because they are saved. You poor souls, groveling under the law. How I do pity you, torn by fear and uncertainty and insecurity. You might still lose out and be lost in the end. Oh, realize your inheritance in grace. Stop struggling to keep saved. Rest in His grace, and then your service will be one of joy and gratitude and thanksgiving, and the effort and the worry you now put forth to try to keep saved, could be used to get others saved."[65]

OUR UNION WITH CHRIST —
HIS RIGHTEOUSNESS COUNTED AS OURS

Because I am "in Christ" and my sin was counted as His, His righteousness is counted as mine. I do not stand today in my own righteousness but in His. If I can lose my salvation then there must be a flaw in His righteousness for it is in this that I stand.

> "But now the righteousness of God without the law is manifested, being witnessed by the law and the prophets; Even the *righteousness of God which is by faith of Jesus Christ unto all and upon all them that believe:* for there is no difference" (Romans 3:21-22).

"If it were man's righteousness, it would be through something man accomplished. But it is *God's righteousness;* it is apart from our right-doing — that is, law keeping altogether; for keeping law would be the only way man could get a righteousness of his own.

"But the moment we mention righteousness here, people can hardly be restrained from the notion that they are to have a new *quality* bestowed upon them. Since they have themselves lost this quality of righteousness, they are anxious to get it back — the consciousness of it. But this is really self-righteousness — and that at its worst."[66]

> "*Being justified freely* by His grace through the redemption that is in Christ Jesus" (Romans 3:24).

William R. Newell translates this verse: "*Being declared righteous* giftwise by His grace through the redemption that is in Christ Jesus."[67]

"Being declared [or accounted] righteous — Justification, or accounting righteous, is God's reckoning to one who believes the whole work and effect before Him of the perfect redemption of Christ. The word never means to make one righteous, or holy; but to account one righteous. Justification is not a change wrought by God in us, but a change of our relation to God."[68]

> "Whom God hath set forth to be a propitiation through faith in His blood, *to declare His righteousness for the remission of sins* that are past, through the forbearance of God; To declare, I say, at this time *His righteousness:* that He might be just, and the *justifier of him which believeth in Jesus*" (Romans 3:25-26).

> "Now to him that worketh is the reward not reckoned of grace, but of debt. But to him that worketh not, but believeth on Him that justifieth the ungodly, *his faith is counted for righteousness*" (Romans 4:4-5).

"God accounts righteous the believing *ungodly as such;* not those who are first to be in any wise 'changed,' and *then* reckoned righteous; not those to whom certain 'merits' of Christ are to be given, so that they are thereby righteous — not at all. But the *believing ungodly* are to be reckoned righteous — while they are *still ungodly:* it is that fact that makes the gospel!

"Justification is God's reckoning a man righteous who has no righteousness, because God is operating wholly upon another basis, even the work of Christ. If Christ fully bore sin for man, and has been raised up by God, a believing man has reckoned to him by God all that infinite work of Christ!"[69]

> "Even as David also describeth the blessedness of the man, *unto whom God imputeth righteousness without works,* Saying, Blessed are they whose iniquities are forgiven, and whose sins are covered. Blessed is the man to whom the Lord will not impute sin" (Romans 4:6-8).

God imputes righteousness to us (counts it as ours) without works. What a wonderful truth!

> "For if by one man's offence death reigned by one; much more they which receive abundance of grace and of the *gift of righteousness* shall reign in life by one, Jesus Christ" (Romans 5:17).

"Righteousness" is a gift. It is not earned nor is it kept by our works. It is *His* righteousness that is counted as ours.

"Therefore as by the offence of one judgment came upon all men to condemnation; even so by the righteousness of one the free gift came upon all men unto justification of life. For as by one man's disobedience many were made sinners, *so by the obedience of one shall many be made righteous*" (Romans 5:18-19).

"What shall we say then? That the Gentiles, which followed not after righteousness, have attained to righteousness, even the *righteousness which is of faith.* But Israel, which followed after the law of righteousness, hath not attained to the law of righteousness. Wherefore? Because they sought it not by faith, but as it were by the works of the law. For they stumbled at that stumblingstone" (Romans 9:30-32).

True "righteousness" is obtained by faith. Israel tried to get it by works but they sought it in the wrong way. How are you seeking it?

"For they being ignorant of *God's righteousness,* and going about to establish their own righteousness, have not submitted themselves unto the *righteousness of God. For Christ is the end of the law for righteousness to every one that believeth*" (Romans 10:3-4).

Oh, that men could really believe what God says here, "Christ is the *end of the law for righteousness* to everyone that believeth." But many still struggle to keep their "righteousness" by keeping the law (works). What a useless struggle for "all our righteousnesses are as filthy rags" (Isaiah 64:6). One "in Christ" stands in God's righteousness. It is counted as his.

"But of Him are ye in Christ Jesus, who of God is made unto us wisdom, and *righteousness,* and sanctification, and redemption" (1 Corinthians 1:30).

"For He hath made Him to be sin for us, who knew no sin; that we might be made the *righteousness of God in Him*" (2 Corinthians 5:21).

William R. Newell writes: "The saints are said to be the righteousness of God, in Christ. Of course self-righteousness simply shrivels before a verse like this! All is in Christ: we are *in* Christ — one with Him!"[70]

"Does Christ need something yet, that He may stand in acceptance with God? Then do I need something — for I am in Christ, and He alone is my righteousness. If He stands in full, eternal acceptance, then do I also for I am now in Him alone, having died with Him to my old place in Adam."[71]

> "I do not frustrate the grace of God: for *if righteousness come by the law, then Christ is dead in vain*" (*Galatians 2:21*).

> "Even as Abraham *believed God, and it was accounted to him for righteousness*" (Galatians 3:6).

> "Is the law then against the promises of God? God forbid: for if there had been a law given which could have given life, verily righteousness should have been by the law. But the scripture hath concluded all under sin, that the promise by faith of Jesus Christ might be given to them that believe" (Galatians 3:21-22).

> "And be found in Him, *not having mine own righteousness, which is of the law, but that which is through the faith of Christ, the righteousness which is of God by faith*" (Philippians 3:9).

> "*Not by works of righteousness which we have done*, but according to His mercy He saved us, by the washing of regeneration, and renewing of the Holy Ghost; Which He shed on us abundantly through Jesus Christ our Saviour; That being *justified by His grace*, we should be made heirs according to the hope of eternal life" (Titus 3:5-7).

> "And the *work of righteousness* shall be peace; and the *effect of righteousness* quietness and *assurance for ever*" (Isaiah 32:17).

Dr. H.A. Ironside writes: "If my acceptance depended on my growth in grace I could never have settled peace. It would be egotism of the worst kind to consider myself so holy that I could be satisfactory to God on the ground of my personal experience. But when I see that 'He hath made us accepted in the beloved,' every doubt is banished. My soul is at peace. I have quietness and assurance forever. I know now that only:

> That which can shake the cross,
> Can shake the peace it gave;
> Which tells me Christ has never died
> Nor ever left the grave.

"As long as these great unchanging verities remain, my peace is unshaken, my confidence is secure, I have 'assurance forever.' "[72]

"I will greatly rejoice in the LORD, my soul shall be joyful in my God; for He hath clothed me with the garments of salvation, *He hath covered me with the robe of righteousness,* as a bridegroom decketh himself with ornaments, and as a bride adorneth herself with her jewels" (Isaiah 61:10).

OUR UNION WITH CHRIST — OUR ETERNAL FUTURE LINKED TO THAT OF CHRIST

Because I am "in Christ" my eternal future is linked with that of Christ. If He can be lost so can I. If He cannot be lost then neither can I.

"And if children, then *heirs; heirs of God,* and *joint-heirs with Christ;* if so be that we suffer with Him, that we may be also glorified together" (Romans 8:17).

I am an heir of God and a "joint-heir" with Christ. This is almost beyond our human comprehension. *For me to be a joint-heir with Christ means that all that is Christ's for eternity is mine for I am a joint-heir. It means that all that God has prepared for Christ He has prepared for me also for I am a joint-heir.*

"Wherefore thou art no more a servant, but a son; and if a son, then an *heir of God through Christ*" (Galatians 4:7).

"Beloved, now are we the sons of God, and it doth not yet appear what we shall be: but we know that, *when He shall appear, we shall be like Him;* for we shall see Him as He is" (1 John 3:2).

We are *now* "sons of God" and when Christ comes for His own *we shall be "like Him." My future is linked with His.*

"For ye are dead, and your life is hid with Christ in God. *When Christ, who is our life, shall appear, then shall ye also appear with Him in glory*" (Colossians 3:3-4).

"In My Father's house are many mansions: if it were not so, I would have told you. I go to prepare a place for you. And if I go and prepare a place for you, *I will come again, and receive you unto Myself; that where I am, there ye may be* also" (John 14:2-3).

What a glorious truth — where Christ is, there will we be also! Our future is linked with His.

"Father, I will that they also, whom Thou hast given Me, *be with Me where I am:* that they may behold My glory, which Thou hast given Me: for Thou lovedst Me before the foundation of the world" (John 17:24).

"Husbands, love your wives, even as Christ also loved the church, and gave Himself for it; That He might sanctify and cleanse it with the washing of water by the word, That He might present it to Himself a glorious church, not having spot, or wrinkle, or any such thing; but that it should be holy and without blemish" (Ephesians 5:25-27).

"Wherefore, my brethren, ye also are become dead to the law by the body of Christ; *that ye should be married to another,* even to Him who is raised from the dead, that we should bring forth fruit unto God" (Romans 7:4).

"Let us be glad and rejoice, and give honour to Him: for the marriage of the Lamb is come, and *His wife* hath made herself ready" (Revelation 19:7).

"For the Lord Himself shall descend from heaven with a shout, with the voice of the archangel, and with the trump of God: and the dead in Christ shall rise first: Then we which are alive and remain shall be caught up together with them in the clouds, to meet the Lord in the air: and *so shall we ever be with the Lord*" (1 Thessalonians 4:16-17).

"To him that overcometh *will I grant to sit with Me in My throne,* even as I also overcame, and am set down with My Father in His throne" (Revelation 3:21).

This is for all true believers for he that "overcometh" is he that is "born of God," "that believeth that Jesus is the Son of God" (1 John 5:4-5).

> "For whom He did foreknow, He also did *predestinate to be conformed to the image of His Son,* that He might be the firstborn among many brethren" (Romans 8:29).

All who are saved were "foreknown" by God before the foundation of the world (1 Peter 1:20; Ephesians 1:4); and all whom He foreknew He "predestinated" "to be conformed to the image of His Son."

> "For our conversation is in heaven; from whence also we look for the Saviour, the Lord Jesus Christ: *Who shall change our vile body, that it may be fashioned like unto His glorious body,* according to the working whereby He is able even to subdue all things unto Himself" (Philippians 3:20-21).

18

SECURITY AND THE APPEALS FOR GODLY LIVING

The appeals in the Bible for godly living are not based on a threatened loss of salvation but rather on all that we have in Christ and our security in Him. To attempt to get a person to live a good life and not to sin by threatening him with the loss of salvation is unscriptural.

One does not put his money in a bank unless he is quite sure it will be secure, nor will one often invest his life as a sacrifice and work for God unless he knows that his investment will be secure.

"Many of the strongest appeals in the Bible for a pure, holy, righteous, and godly life are based on statements which definitely teach the eternal security of the believer."[73]

Suppose a teacher gave out a number of assignments for extra credit and informed the pupils that they could raise their grades by doing them. Suppose she also stated that they had to score 100 per cent on every regular test or else they would fail the course and the extra credit work would be in vain. Would there be much incentive for doing extra work? No! One slip on a regular test and all the time spent on extra work would be worthless. To threaten a believer with the loss of salvation takes away much of the incentive for godly living. If a believer spent years in faithful service for the Lord and then slipped and as a result lost his salvation — all his labor would be in vain. God, however, says that we "know" that our "labour is not in vain in the Lord" (1 Corinthians 15:58).

> "I beseech you therefore, brethren, *by the mercies of God,* that ye present your bodies a living sacrifice, holy, acceptable unto God, which is your reasonable service. And be not conformed to this world: but be ye transformed by the renewing of your mind, that ye may prove what is that good, and acceptable, and perfect, will of God" (Romans 12:1-2).

This plea that we present our bodies a living sacrifice is not based on a threatened loss of salvation but rather on the "mercies of God"; just the opposite! The "therefore" refers back to these "mercies of God" which are named by Paul in the foregoing chapters of Romans:

Justification — Declared righteous before God by faith (Romans 3:28; 5:1).

Identification with Christ — "In Christ" and therefore dead with Him to sin and the law, and risen with Him to newness of life (Romans 6:1-10):

Under Grace, Not Law — (Romans 6:14)

Indwelling of the Spirit — (Romans 8:1-27)

Help in Infirmity — (Romans 8:26)

Divine Election — (Romans 8:33)

Coming Glory — (Romans 8:18)

No Separation Possible — (Romans 8:35-39)

God's Faithfulness — as shown by His dealings with national Israel (Romans 9—11).[74]

> "Know ye not that your bodies *are the members of Christ?* shall I then take the members of Christ, and make them the members of an harlot? God forbid" (1 Corinthians 6:15).

The appeal here is made on the basis that our bodies *are the members of Christ.*

> "What? know ye not that your body is the temple of the Holy Ghost which is in you, which ye have of God, and ye are not your own? For ye are bought with a price: therefore glorify God in your body, and in your spirit, which are God's" (1 Corinthians 6:19-20).

This appeal to glorify God is based upon the facts "that the Holy Spirit indwells the believer and that Christ paid the price for his redemption"[75] and that his body and spirit are God's.

> "I therefore, the prisoner of the Lord, beseech you that ye walk worthy of the vocation wherewith ye are called, With all lowliness and meekness, with longsuffering, forbearing one another in love; Endeavouring to keep the unity of the Spirit in the bond of peace" (Ephesians 4:1-3).

The "therefore" here refers back to what has been said in the previous chapters as a basis for the appeal to "walk worthy." Is this a threatened loss of salvation? Far from it. These chapters show our standing in Christ and all that we have in Him:

"Chosen in Him before the foundation of the world" (Ephesians 1:4)

"We have redemption" (Ephesians 1:7)

"We have obtained an inheritance" (Ephesians 1:11)

"Sealed with the Holy Spirit" (Ephesians 1:13)

"Made us to sit together in the heavenlies" (Ephesians 2:6)

"Fellowcitizens with the saints" (Ephesians 2:19)

"An habitation of God through the Spirit" (Ephesians 2:22)

"The love of Christ" (Ephesians 3:19)

His "power worketh in us" (Ephesians 3:20)

Holy living, then, is a result of the teaching of the security which we have in Christ.

> "As ye know how we exhorted and comforted and charged every one of you, as a father doth his children, That ye would walk worthy of God, who hath called you unto His kingdom and glory" (1 Thessalonians 2:11-12).

This appeal for a "walk worthy of God" is made as a father exhorts, comforts, and charges his children. It is a far cry from what we hear today from many pulpits: scoldings and threatened loss of salvation.

Notice also that God *hath* called us unto His kingdom and glory and according to Romans 11:29 the "calling of God is without repentance." It will not be taken back.

"For the grace of God that bringeth salvation hath appeared to all men, Teaching us that, denying ungodliness and worldly lusts, we should live soberly, righteously, and godly, in this present world" (Titus 2:11-12).

Notice what it is that teaches us to live "soberly, righteously, and godly," and to deny "ungodliness and worldly lusts." It is the *"grace of God"* that does so. There is no threatened loss of salvation here.

"If ye then be risen with Christ, seek those things which are above, where Christ sitteth on the right hand of God. Set your affection on things above, not on things on the earth. For ye are dead, and your life is hid with Christ in God" (Colossians 3:1-3).

Here the appeal is that we "seek those things which are above" not because we might lose our salvation, but because we are risen with Christ; because our life is hid with Christ in God.

Security, not fear, brings about godly living!

"Be ye not unequally yoked together with unbelievers: for what fellowship hath righteousness with unrighteousness? and what communion hath light with darkness? And what concord hath Christ with Belial? or what part hath he that believeth with an infidel? And what agreement hath the temple of God with idols? for ye are the temple of the living God; as God hath said, I will dwell in them, and walk in them; and I will be their God, and they shall be My people" (2 Corinthians 6:14-16).

This appeal that believers be "not unequally yoked together with unbelievers" is based on the facts:

That we *are* "righteousness" (in Christ)
That we *are* "light" (in Christ)
That we *are* "the temple of the living God."

These things are true of us now.

"Mortify therefore your members which are upon the earth;

fornication, uncleanness, inordinate affection, evil concupiscence, and covetousness, which is idolatry" (Colossians 3:5).

The "therefore" refers back to verse 4: "When Christ, *who is our life*, shall appear, then shall ye also appear with Him in glory."

The basis for this appeal for godly living, then, is the fact that we "shall" appear in glory. This is assurance, not fear of loss!

"It is a definite, unconditional statement that connects the believer with Christ in glory that is the reason given as the incentive to purity. To teach that one who is saved might not appear with Christ in glory [that is, be lost] and that possibly because of one of the very sins enumerated, is to take away from such an one the incentive to purity that God has caused to be written down for his special help when he is about to sin."[76]

"Wherefore laying aside all malice, and all guile, and hypocrisies, and envies, and all evil speakings, As newborn babes, desire the sincere milk of the word, that ye may grow thereby" (1 Peter 2:1-2).

This appeal is based on the fact that we are born again "not of corruptible seed, but of incorruptible" (1 Peter 1:23). It is our security in Christ upon which the appeal is based.

"If the fact of the unending nature of the new life of the saved one (which means that he is eternally secure) is denied, then there is very little left, if anything, upon which to appeal to saved people to lay aside all these things and to cultivate an appetite for God's Word. Nothing can more stimulate a desire for knowledge of God's Word than a clear understanding of the fact that one is born again of incorruptible seed and is certain of being in glory with Christ."[77]

"Therefore, my beloved brethren, be ye stedfast, unmoveable, always abounding in the work of the Lord, forasmuch as ye know that your labour is not in vain in the Lord" (1 Corinthians 15:58).

This appeal is based on the fact of the "rapture" which has been described in the preceding verses (1 Corinthians 15:51-57) when Christ comes for His own and when this "corruptible" body will "put on incorruption." It is also based on the fact that we *know* that our labor is not in vain in the Lord.

If we could lose our salvation, this appeal would lose its force, for we could not know that our labor would not be in vain. Our "security" is also the basis for this appeal.

> "Ye are all the children of light, and the children of the day: we are not of the night, nor of darkness. Therefore let us not sleep, as do others; but let us watch and be sober. For they that sleep sleep in the night; and they that be drunken are drunken in the night. But let us, who are of the day, be sober, putting on the breastplate of faith and love; and for an helmet, the hope of salvation. For God hath not appointed us to wrath, but to obtain salvation by our Lord Jesus Christ, Who died for us, that, whether we wake or sleep, we should live together with Him" (1 Thessalonians 5:5-10).

This appeal not to sleep but be sober "putting on the breastplate of faith and love," etc., is based on the truths that we *are* the *children of light,* and the *children of the day* (verses 5,8) and that *"God hath not appointed us to wrath"* (verse 9). There is no threat of the loss of salvation here but rather an admonition based on what we are and have in Christ.

> "Forasmuch as ye know that ye were not redeemed with corruptible things, as silver and gold, from your vain conversation received by tradition from your fathers; But with the precious blood of Christ, as of a lamb without blemish and without spot: Who verily was foreordained before the foundation of the world, but was manifest in these last times for you, Who by Him do believe in God, that raised Him up from the dead, and gave Him glory; that your faith and hope might be in God. Seeing ye have purified your souls in obeying the truth through the Spirit unto unfeigned love of the brethren, see that ye love one another with a pure heart fervently" (1 Peter 1:18-22).

We are to "love one another with a pure heart fervently" because we *know* that we are redeemed with "the precious blood of Christ." Again, there is no threatened loss of salvation here but an appeal based upon the fact of our redemption.

> "Beloved, now are we the sons of God, and it doth not yet appear what we shall be: but we know that, when He shall appear, we

shall be like Him; for we shall see Him as He is. And every man that hath this hope in Him purifieth himself, even as He is pure" (1 John 3:2-3).

Notice who it is that "purifieth himself." It is the one who is *now* a Son of God, who *knows* that when Jesus comes he will be "like Him." The word "hope" in the Bible is not used of something that may or may not happen but of a certainty that has not yet come to pass. *The one who purifies himself is the one who is eternally secure in Christ.*

"Therefore, my brethren dearly beloved and longed for, my joy and crown, so stand fast in the Lord, my dearly beloved" (Philippians 4:1).

This appeal to "stand fast" is based on the truths found in the preceding verses:

"Our conversation [citizenship] is in Heaven." (Philippians 3:20)

He "shall change our vile body, that it may be fashioned like unto His glorious body."

Is this in any way a threat that we may lose our salvation? It is not! It is rather assurance.

"For the love of Christ constraineth us; because we thus judge, that if one died for all, then were all dead: And that He died for all, that they which live should not henceforth live unto themselves, but unto Him which died for them, and rose again" (2 Corinthians 5:14-15).

It is the "love of Christ" that constrains us. "Therefore, fear of the wrath of God (being lost) cannot be the dynamic of holy and righteous living. Neither can it be said that it is the righteousness or holiness of God that is the constraining influence.

"It is that love that was expressed when Christ died and rose again. It was through that death and resurrection that all old things passed away, yea even the curse and condemnation of the law, and the believer became a new creature in Christ that cannot die. It is that love of God which He manifested when He was in Christ on the cross, reconciling the world unto Himself (2 Corinthians 5:15-19). It is that love of God from which the believer cannot be separated, and which guarantees the eternal security of everyone that has become the object thereof." 78

J. F. Strombeck writes: "Every one of the conditions upon which these various appeals are based is materially weakened, if not entirely destroyed, by the teaching that one who has been saved can be lost, for that denies the unalterable nature of these conditions.

"It would seem, then, that worldliness in the church of today is chargeable to failure to teach the doctrines of the grace of God which are inseparable from the truth of eternal security. As denial of the truth of eternal security makes it impossible to teach these doctrines in their fullness, it follows that those who teach against that truth are contributing to the present state of worldliness in the churches."79

Part 2

ANSWERS TO ARGUMENTS

AGAINST ETERNAL SECURITY

19

ARGUMENTS ABOUT CARELESS LIVING

Some say that teaching the "eternal security" of the believer will cause careless living. They say that if you teach believers that they are eternally secure they will think that it doesn't make any difference how they live. The opposite is really true.

Lewis Sperry Chafer writes, "There is no greater incentive to holiness of life than to know one's own eternal position in Christ Jesus."[80]

"To claim that teaching the doctrine of security will license people to sin is to ignore the mighty revelations of the believer's positions and the effect of these upon the life. It is to ignore the fact of the new divine nature which indwells each child of God. It is to ignore the new dispositions and tendencies flowing out of that new life. It is to ignore the imparted energy of God, 'for it is God which worketh in you both to will and to do of His good pleasure.' It is to challenge every revelation concerning God's plan of dealing with His child."[81]

M. R. DeHaan says, "If you think that salvation by grace encourages sin, then you don't understand grace."[82]

"For, brethren, ye have been called unto liberty; *only use not liberty for an occasion to the flesh,* but by love serve one another" (Galatians 5:13).

The Christian is called to "liberty" (freedom). He is "dead to the law" (Romans 7:4; Galatians 2:19) and therefore free from it. But here we are shown that freedom should not be an excuse to sin, but rather should cause us, in love, to serve one another.

"For the *grace of God* that bringeth salvation hath appeared to all men, Teaching us that, denying ungodliness and worldly lusts, we should live soberly, righteously, and godly, in this present world" (Titus 2:11-12).

It is *not God's holiness, nor His righteousness;* it is *not the law, nor the threat of condemnation* that teaches holy living. *It is the "grace of God" that does so!* It is His "unmerited favor," His giving us salvation apart from our works, that teaches us holy living.

"For we are His workmanship, *created in Christ Jesus unto good works, which God hath before ordained that we should walk in them"* (Ephesians 2:10).

"For He has made us what we are, because He has *created us through our union with Christ Jesus for doing good deeds* which He beforehand planned for us to do" (Ephesians 2:10 Williams).

"Notice the order. He has already told us that we are not saved by our good works (Ephesians 2:8-9), but now says that we must not ignore good works, for one of the purposes for which He has saved us is in order that we might do good works."[83] The great truth here is that *"in Christ"* we are *"new creatures"* with *new natures.* The one who is truly saved does not find in sin the pleasure that he once did before his salvation because he *is* a new creature *"created — unto good works."* He does not do good works because of a threatened loss of salvation, but as a result of salvation, as a result of his union with Christ.

"Whosoever is born of God *doth not commit sin;* for His seed remaineth in him: *and he cannot sin,* because he is born of God. In this the children of God are manifest, and the children of the devil: *whosoever doeth not righteousness is not of God,* neither he that loveth not his brother" (1 John 3:9-10).

What is meant here is not that a Christian cannot sin at all, for this would be a direct contradiction of 1 John 1:8,10, but that he cannot continually practice sin.

"No one who is born of God practices sin" (New American Standard)

"He cannot keep sinning" (Expositor's Greek Testament)

"No one who is born of God makes a practice of sinning" (Williams)

"A born-one of God does not habitually commit sin" (Wuest)

"No one born (begotten) of God [deliberately and knowingly] habitually practices sin" (Amplified Bible)

Why won't a true believer continually practice sin? Not because he is afraid he will lose his salvation but because he cannot "because he is born of God"; because His "seed" *remaineth* in him. (Notice that His "seed" is not withdrawn because of sin but "remaineth" in the believer and it is this that keeps him from continually sinning.)

Anyone who does continually practice sin; that is, he "doeth not righteousness," is *not* a child of God, for one who is born of God *cannot* continually practice sin. This is a result of salvation — not a condition for obtaining salvation.

> "We *know* that whosoever is born of God sinneth not; but he that is begotten of God keepeth himself, and *that wicked one toucheth him not*" (1 John 5:18).

> "We know that no one who is born of God makes a practice of sinning, but the Son who was born of God continues to keep him, and the evil one cannot touch him" (1 John 5:18 Williams).

> "We know [absolutely] that anyone born of God does not [deliberately and knowingly] practise committing sin, but the One Who was begotten of God carefully watches over and protects him — Christ's divine presence within him preserves him against the evil — and the wicked one does not lay hold (get a grip) on him or touch [him]" (1 John 5:18 Amplified Bible).

If one born of God does not make a practice of sinning (and he doesn't) and if the Son of God (Jesus) continues to keep him (and He does) and if the "evil one" cannot touch (grasp or lay hold of) him (and he cannot), then how can a child of God be lost?

> "Let not sin therefore reign in your mortal body, that ye should obey it in the lusts thereof. Neither yield ye your members as instruments of unrighteousness unto sin: but yield yourselves unto God, *as those that are alive from the dead,* and your members as

instruments of righteousness unto God. For *sin shall not have
dominion over you:* for ye are *not* under the law, but under grace.
What then? *shall we sin, because we are not under the law, but
under grace?* God forbid" (Romans 6:12-15).

The pleas against sin and unrighteousness here are not based
on a threatened loss of salvation but rather on the fact that we,
who are saved, are "alive from the dead" spiritually.

The reason that sin will not have dominion over a Christian is
not because he is afraid that he may lose his salvation, but just
the opposite — that he is under "grace" (God's unmerited favor).
Note carefully that it is being under "grace" that keeps sin from
having dominion over us.

Then in verse 15 Paul asks the very same question we hear
raised so often today by those who doubt the security of the
believer. "Shall we sin, because we are not under the law, but
under grace?" Doesn't this sound familiar? "Won't telling a
person that he is under grace, that he is secure in Christ cause
him to sin?" ask those who do not believe in the security of the
believer. Paul answers the question:

"God forbid" (King James Version)

"Never (Williams)

"Certainly not" (Montgomery)

"Away with the thought" (Wuest)

"Be it not thought of" (Newell)[84]

"He that saith he abideth in Him ought himself also so to walk,
even as He walked" (1 John 2:6).

When the Scriptures use the word "abide" in speaking of our
relationship with Christ they are speaking of our fellowship and
communion with Him. One who is "abiding" in Him (maintaining close fellowship with Him) will be walking as He walked.

"A true Christian walk is a reproducing in our lives of the
righteousness which is already ours in Christ."[85]

"But God forbid that I should glory, save in the cross of our Lord

Jesus Christ, by whom the world is crucified unto me, and I unto the world" (Galatians 6:14).

"God forbid. How shall we, that are dead to sin, live any longer therein?" (Romans 6:2)

It is by the cross of Christ that I am crucified to the world and the world to me. I am dead to sin.

A. J. Gordon puts it very well when he says: "The *flesh*, warring against the Spirit, violating every truce with conscience, breaking every covenant which we have made with God — behold, this enemy from whom we cannot flee, has yet received his death wound. Christ put a nail through him when He gave His own body to the smiters. 'And they that are Christ's have crucified the flesh with the affections and lusts.' Wounded unto death, yet struggling for his lost dominion, we shall never be wholly quit of him, till the grave closes over him. But in God's reckoning we are even now delivered. 'Ye are not in the flesh, but in the Spirit.' Upon our natural and guilt-attainted man, justice has executed his death-warrant, and is satisfied. In words traced by the infallible Spirit of truth, we have the record of his decease: '*Ye died*, and your life is hid with Christ in God.' "[86]

20

ARGUMENTS FROM EXPERIENCE

"I know some who have been saved and lost." This is an argument which is often used by those who do not believe in the security of the believer. It is not based upon the Bible but rather upon their experience.

"There are many who profess to be Christians, who take part in religious work, or have joined some church, who have never been saved. Going forward in a revival meeting, weeping or passing through emotional periods, does not constitute being saved. These may and sometimes do accompany salvation, but they are not salvation. It is even possible for men to preach in the Name of Christ without having been saved (Matthew 7:22-23). A moral reformation is not salvation. In fact, it may be quite the opposite because it may be the result of human will power and action and not of God.

"Because man judges the outward being and not the heart, there are many mistakes made in judging persons as saved or unsaved. The doctrine of eternal security has nothing to say about this vast number who only give outward show, but who lack the heart relationship with God."[87]

Here are some verses which we believe are an answer to the argument that says, "I know some who have been saved and lost." Experience is unreliable. Let us rely on the Word of God.

> "Therefore judge nothing before the time, until the Lord come, who both will bring to light the hidden things of darkness, and will make manifest the counsels of the hearts: and then shall every man have praise of God" (1 Corinthians 4:5).

Those who know the Lord can recognize others as Christians by various means:

"By their fruits ye shall know them" (Matthew 7:20)

"If ye have love one to another" (John 13:35)

"If any man love the world, the love of the Father is not in him" (1 John 2:15)

This, however, is quite different from making a positive statement that men are saved or not saved. No man can definitely declare of another that he is either saved or lost. If it becomes obvious that a man, who once appeared to be saved is not saved, it is only proof that he was never saved. It is by "fruit" that we shall know them.

> "Nevertheless the foundation of God standeth sure, having this seal, The Lord knoweth them that are His. And, Let every one that nameth the name of Christ depart from iniquity" (2 Timothy 2:19).

God knows them that are His. We may not know for certain concerning one's salvation but God does.

> "But the Lord said unto Samuel, Look not on his countenance, or on the height of his stature; because I have refused him: for the Lord seeth not as man seeth; for man looketh on the outward appearance, but the Lord looketh on the heart" (1 Samuel 16:7).

Because man can only look at the outward appearance of another and not at the heart he cannot state positively that any man is saved or lost.

> "Not every one that saith unto Me, Lord, Lord, shall enter into the kingdom of heaven; but he that doeth the will of My Father which is in heaven. Many will say to Me in that day, Lord, Lord, have we not prophesied in Thy name? and in Thy name have cast out devils? and in Thy name done many wonderful works? And then will I profess unto them, I never knew you: depart from Me, ye that work iniquity" (Matthew 7:21-23).

These verses show very definitely that many that appear to know the Lord actually do not. Jesus does not say to them, "I once knew you, but you are now lost," but rather, "I *never* knew you." They were never really saved.

"You see, it does not inevitably follow that one who has been active in Christian work, even preached and wrought miracles and cast out devils, is saved. Before men he was accepted, but God saw the heart."[88]

> "Now we command you, brethren, in the name of our Lord Jesus Christ, that ye withdraw yourselves from every brother that walketh disorderly, and not after the tradition which he received of us" (2 Thessalonians 3:6).

Here some who are walking disorderly are called "brothers." A Christian may slip into sin but he is still a "brother." Sin will break his close fellowship with God and even with other believers but he is still saved.

> "And if any man obey not our word by this epistle, note that man, and have no company with him, that he may be ashamed. Yet count him not as an enemy, but admonish him as a brother" (2 Thessalonians 3:14-15).

Here again one walking in sin is to be admonished as a "brother." We cannot know positively that he is a brother and should withdraw from him. If he is a brother he should be ashamed.

> "But now I have written unto you not to keep company, if any ... that is called a brother be a fornicator, or covetous, or an idolater, or a railer, or a drunkard, or an extortioner; with such an one no not to eat" (1 Corinthians 5:11).

This does not say that he *is* a brother but that he is *called* a brother. He may not know the Lord at all or he may be a brother in a backslidden condition.

Williams translates "any so-called brother."

> "And delivered *just* Lot, vexed with the filthy conversation of the wicked: For that *righteous* man dwelling among them, in seeing and hearing, vexed his *righteous* soul from day to day with their unlawful deeds" (2 Peter 2:7-8).

Lot would, by his life, certainly have appeared to be lost but "God looketh on the heart." Lot is said to be *"just," "righteous."* "Who is right, God or man? *No modern case quoted as proof against eternal security has looked more hopeless than Lot.* Yet men who are teachers of God's Word say, 'We know from our own experience that persons who have been saved can be lost.' "[89]

> "And we believe and are sure that thou art that Christ, the Son of the living God. Jesus answered them, Have not I chosen you twelve, and one of you is a devil?" (John 6: 69-70)

Peter here is speaking for all the disciples — "We believe." Jesus, however, immediately says that one of them "is a devil." To the other disciples Judas appeared to be righteous. "There is not the slightest record of any of the other eleven mistrusting him."[90] Jesus saw his heart. Human experience is not reliable.

> "They went out from us, but they were not of us; for if they had been of us, they would no doubt have continued with us: but they went out, that they might be made manifest that they were not all of us" (1 John 2:19).

> "They have gone out from our own number, but they did not really belong to us; for if they had, they would have stayed with us. It was to show that none of those who went out really belonged to us" (1 John 2:19 Williams).

Those spoken of here, no doubt, appeared to many to be saved, but the Bible says, *"they were not of us."* Many today point to people who at one time appeared to be saved but then go out and live in sin. This verse certainly applies to them. *"If they had been of us, they would have continued with us"* (The words "no doubt" are not in the Greek text).

> "Examine yourselves, whether ye be in the faith; prove your own selves. Know ye not your own selves, how that Jesus Christ is in you, except ye be reprobates?" (2 Corinthians 13:5)

Examine *your* faith. Is it real or is it counterfeit? Is Christ in you or are you just pretending? Many people are deceived by Satan into thinking that they are saved when they have never really seen themselves as lost sinners and accepted Christ as Saviour.

J. F. Strombeck writes: *"Anyone who definitely makes the statement concerning someone, that he has been saved and is now lost, is making a double judgment whereby he intrudes himself into the position of God."*[91]

"It is placing fallible and finite judgment and reasoning of man above God's infinite and infallible Word." [92]

21

IF I STOP BELIEVING

Some who do not believe in the eternal security of the believer say that it is true that we cannot lose our salvation by works, but they ask the question, "What if I stop believing?" "If salvation is mine by believing," they say, "then I can lose it by ceasing to believe." This argument has already been answered in almost every section of Part 1 of this book but since it is so often used, this section will deal especially with verses that show that a truly born-again believer cannot lose his salvation even by ceasing to believe.

> "Verily, verily, I say unto you, He that heareth My word, and believeth on Him that sent Me, *hath everlasting life,* and *shall not come into condemnation;* but is passed from death unto life" (John 5:24).

The one who believes has (present tense) *everlasting* life. The word "everlasting" describes the length of this life. If I could lose this everlasting life, which I now have, by ceasing to believe, then it wasn't everlasting.

This verse also states that one who has this everlasting life "shall not come into condemnation." If one does come into condemnation by ceasing to believe (loses his salvation) then this verse is not true.

See also John 3:36; John 3:14-15; John 6:47; 1 John 5:11-13.

> "And I give unto them eternal life; and they *shall never perish,* neither shall any man pluck them out of My hand" (John 10:28).

Here Jesus says that those to whom He gives eternal life "shall never perish." If by ceasing to believe they could lose their salvation, then they *could* perish and this would not be true.

See also Romans 8:1; John 3:18; John 3:15-16.

> "These things have I written unto you that believe on the name of the Son of God; *that ye may know* that ye have eternal life, and that ye may believe on the name of the Son of God" (1 John 5:13).

Here it is stated that we may *know* that we have eternal life. If one who has eternal life could lose by ceasing to believe then he could *not* know and this verse would not be true.

The Bible also states that we may know certain other things — in 1 John 3:2; 2 Corinthians 5:1; 1 Corinthians 15:58; and 2 Corinthians 4:14. None of these things could truly be known if one could in any way lose his salvation.

> "Therefore if any man be in Christ, he is a new creature: old things are passed away; behold, all things are become new" (2 Corinthians 5:17).

Will the "new creature" die if the believer stops believing? See also Galatians 6:15; Ephesians 2:10; 4:24.

> "Being born again, not of corruptible seed, but of incorruptible, by the word of God, which liveth and abideth for ever" (1 Peter 1:23).

Every true believer has been *"born again."* He has become a *"son of God."* He has been born of *"incorruptible seed."* That which is corruptible can die but that which is "incorruptible" *cannot die.* Therefore the one who is now a "son of God" will *always* be. God will chasten him when he is disobedient but he will always be in His family.

See also John 3:3,6; John 1:12-13; Titus 3:5; Romans 8:16-17; Galatians 4:7; Galatians 3:26; Hebrews 12:6-8.

> "Now therefore ye are no more strangers and foreigners, but fellowcitizens with the saints, and of the household of God" (Ephesians 2:19).

"For our conversation is in heaven; from whence also we look for the Saviour, the Lord Jesus Christ" (Philippians 3:20).

We are already citizens of Heaven. God has enrolled us there. If we could lose our salvation by ceasing to believe then God made a mistake in making us citizens.

See also 2 Corinthians 5:1; Hebrews 12:22-23.

"When Christ, who is our life, shall appear, then shall ye also appear with Him in glory" (Colossians 3:4).

The believer "shall" appear with Him in glory. There is no question about it. It is stated as a fact. If a believer could lose his salvation by ceasing to believe or in any other way it could not be stated this way.

There are other things that God says "shall" be in Romans 5:8-9; 5:17; 8:11; 8:18; 1 Corinthians 1:8; 15:49; 15:51; 2 Corinthians 4:14; 1 John 3:2. If there were even a remote possibility that the believer could lose his salvation it could not be stated that these things "shall" be.

"Being confident of this very thing, that He which hath begun a good work in you *will perform it until the day of Jesus Christ*" (Philippians 1:6).

This verse and Colossians 3:3; Romans 8:31-32; Hebrews 7:24-25; Hebrews 13:5; Romans 8:35-39; John 6:39-40; 6:44; 17:11; 17:20-21; Hebrews 10:14; Romans 11:29; 1 Corinthians 1:4-9; John 6:37; 1 Peter 1:3-5; 2 Timothy 1:12; 4:18; 2 Thessalonians 3:3; Jude 24-25; John 10:27-29; all show conclusively that, *once a person is truly saved, God keeps him. God will not let him be lost.*

"According as He hath chosen us in Him *before the foundation of the world,* that we should be holy and without blame before Him in love" (Ephesians 1:4).

God chose us, picked us out, before the foundation of the world. He, in His infinite wisdom and foreknowledge, knew all about us way back then. If He knew that we would cease to believe and thus lose our salvation then why did He choose us?

See also Isaiah 46:9-10; Acts 15:18; Psalm 139:16; John 2:24-25; 1 Peter 1:2; Romans 8:29-30; 2 Timothy 1:9; Romans 9:23-24.

> "In whom ye also trusted, after that ye heard the word of truth, the gospel of your salvation: in whom also after that ye believed, ye were sealed with that holy Spirit of promise, Which is the earnest of our inheritance until the redemption of the purchased possession, unto the praise of His glory" (Ephesians 1:13-14).

Can the believer break the seal of the Holy Spirit by ceasing to believe, when God says that seal is *"until the redemption of the purchased possession"*?

See also 2 Corinthians 1:22; Ephesians 4:30; Romans 8:9-11; John 14:16-17; 1 Corinthians 6:19; 1 John 2:27.

22

PASSAGES USED TO TEACH

THAT WE MAY LOSE OUR SALVATION

There are a number of passages in the Bible which may appear on the surface to teach that a "saved one" may be lost. We believe, however, that a closer study of these passages will show that they are in perfect harmony with the overwhelming weight of Scripture which teaches the security of the believer.

J. F. Strombeck writes: "The basic principle of Bible study and interpretation is that *the Bible is one great, harmonious presentation of truth and that each part must harmonize with every other part and with the whole. The great truths concerning sin and condemnation, and grace and eternal life, are outlines to which all else must conform. Therefore the doctrines of sin and of the grace of God are the background against which individual verses must be examined. If there is an apparent meaning that contradicts these great doctrines, then it is necessary to seek some other meaning. Even if no other meaning seems possible, such a verse or even several such cannot be made to annul all that is taught by the whole body of harmonious truth which outweighs such individual verses a thousand-fold."*[93]

We believe that the doctrine of eternal security applies to individual believers of the dispensation of grace in which we live. Some of the passages quoted in this section are written about those under "law" or in some other dispensation. Some are written about nations and do not apply to individuals; some about local churches. Some are written concerning the chastening or even the death of believers, but this is not the loss of salvation or condemnation to eternal punishment. Some passages quoted are taken out of context. Some are written about unbelievers and misapplied. Some are written about those who appear to be believers but are not. Some are just misinterpreted.

After each passage quoted we have attempted to answer the argument that it teaches that a believer may be lost.

Use the Scripture Reference Index in the back of this book to find comments on particular passages that may trouble you.

> "But of the tree of the knowledge of good and evil, thou shalt not eat of it: for in the day that thou eatest thereof thou shalt surely die" (Genesis 2:17).

Read also Genesis 3.

It is said by some who do not believe in the security of the believer that Adam and Eve were in the grace of God spiritually and every other way before the fall, but through sin lost that position in grace and had to be redeemed again.

Before the fall Adam and Eve needed no redemption or salvation for they had no sin. It was because of sin that redemption and salvation became necessary. Adam and Eve did not lose their salvation by eating of the tree of the knowledge of good and evil for they never had salvation until after the fall. They did not need to be saved from the penalty of sin until they had sinned. It is wrong to say that they had to be redeemed again after the fall for they had never been redeemed before the fall nor did they need to be.

"Eternal security" applies to one who has truly been saved from the penalty of sin through the shed blood of Christ at Calvary.

> "Not as Cain, who was of that wicked one, and slew his brother. And wherefore slew he him? Because his own works were evil, and his brother's righteous" (1 John 3:12).

Read also Genesis 4:1-24 and Jude 11.

It is argued that Cain refused all offers of God's grace and was lost.

Cain may well have been lost for the Bible nowhere says he ever accepted God's way of salvation. His offering of the fruit of the ground shows either a woeful ignorance or a deliberate defiance of God's requirement of the shedding of blood. The Bible also says that Cain "was of that wicked one." Eternal security does not apply to one who was never saved.

"And Samuel said unto Saul, I will not return with thee: for thou hast rejected the word of the Lord, and the Lord hath rejected thee from being king over Israel" (1 Samuel 15:26).

"But the Spirit of the Lord departed from Saul, and an evil spirit from the Lord troubled him" (1 Samuel 16:14).

"So Saul died for his transgression which he committed against the Lord, even against the word of the Lord, which he kept not, and also for asking counsel of one that had a familiar spirit, to enquire of it; And enquired not of the Lord: therefore He slew him, and turned the kingdom unto David the son of Jesse" (1 Chronicles 10:13-14).

It is stated by some that these verses show that Saul lost his salvation. These verses were written under "law" and therefore do not apply to one in the dispensation of grace. Even so, however, there is nothing said of the loss of Saul's eternal salvation. In fact, in 1 Samuel 28:19 God allowed Samuel who was dead to speak with Saul and he told him that "to morrow shalt thou and thy sons be with me." This appears to indicate that Saul went to paradise.

Because of Saul's sin he was rejected from being king over Israel (1 Samuel 15:26). To be rejected as king does not mean that he had lost his salvation. Some may say, however, that the fact that the Spirit of God departed from Saul is proof that he lost his salvation (1 Samuel 16:14). In the Old Testament times the Holy Spirit was given to men to empower them for a certain service for God and was at times withdrawn (Judges 3:10; 6:34; 11:29; 13:25; 14:6,19; 15:14,19). Under grace the Holy Spirit comes to dwell with us "for ever" (John 14:16-17) and will not be taken from us (Ephesians 1:13-14; 4:30; 2 Corinthians 1:22; Romans 8:9-11; 1 Corinthians 6:19). (See notes on "Indwelt and Sealed By the Holy Spirit.")

Even in the case of Saul the Holy Spirit came upon him after He departed from him (1 Samuel 19:23).

Saul died because of his sin but physical death is not the same as an eternal loss of salvation.

> "And the Lord was angry with Solomon, because his heart was turned from the Lord God of Israel, which had appeared unto him twice, And had commanded him concerning this thing, that he should not go after other gods: but he kept not that which the Lord commanded. Wherefore the Lord said unto Solomon, Forasmuch as this is done of thee, and thou hast not kept My covenant and My statutes, which I have commanded thee, I will surely rend the kingdom from thee, and [I] will give it to thy servant" (1 Kings 11:9-11).

Read the entire passage — 1 Kings 11:1-11.

This was written concerning one during the dispensation of law and does not apply to this dispensation of grace. God, however, does not say that Solomon was lost. Taking away his kingdom on this earth is not the same as condemning him eternally.

> "Aaron shall be gathered unto his people: for he shall not enter into the land which I have given unto the children of Israel, because ye rebelled against My word at the water of Meribah" (Numbers 20:24).

Because of sin Aaron was not allowed to enter the promised land and died. Physical death, however, is not the same as the eternal loss of salvation.

Many other Israelites also died as a result of sin and it is argued by some that they lost their salvation. We must remember that even some of God's greatest servants died as a result of sin, but death is only the end of this present life in our mortal bodies and not eternal condemnation.

The following is a list of others who died as a result of sin, but nothing is said about any loss of eternal life:

Israelites who complained and were consumed by fire (Numbers 11:1-2);

Israelites who desired flesh rather than manna and were

smitten by a plague (Numbers 11:31-34);

All Israel but Caleb and Joshua (Numbers 14:1-30);

Korah, Dathan, and Abiram and their families whom the earth opened and swallowed (Numbers 16:1-34);

250 Israelites who offered incense and were consumed by fire (Numbers 16:35);

14,700 Israelites who died by plague because they murmured against Moses and Aaron (Numbers 16:41-50);

Israelites who died because of the fiery serpents (Numbers 21:5-9);

Achan and his sons who were stoned (Joshua 7:11-26);

Samson (Judges 16:30);

Even Moses died because of sin and was not allowed to enter the promised land (Numbers 27:12-14; Deuteronomy 1:37; 34:4-5).

In all of these cases physical death is involved, not the loss of salvation.

> "Again, When a righteous man doth turn from his righteousness, and commit iniquity, and I lay a stumblingblock before him, he shall die: because thou hast not given him warning, he shall die in his sin, and his righteousness which he hath done shall not be remembered; but his blood will I require at thine hand" (Ezekiel 3:20).

Read Ezekiel 3:17-21.

This passage was written under the dispensation of law and cannot therefore be applied to the dispensation of grace in which we live.

The Lord in this passage tells Ezekiel that He made him a "watchman unto the house of Israel" (Ezekiel 3:17). As one appointed of God, Ezekiel has a responsibility to warn the wicked and the righteous who are committing iniquity, particularly in Jerusalem, to turn from their wickedness or face the judgment of God. The time concerned is after the original conquest of Jerusalem by Nebuchadnezzar (2 Kings 24:10-19) when

Zedekiah was made king, and before the conquest and destruction of Jerusalem ten years later as a result of the rebellion of Zedekiah (2 Kings 25). The warning given by Ezekiel to those in iniquity is that they face death at the hand of the armies of Nebuchadnezzar (physical death). This is pictured in the prophecy of Ezekiel 9.

Even this passage under law is not a threatened loss of salvation but of physical death. This passage as every passage must be interpreted in its context, considering to whom it was written, when, and for what purpose.

Today, under grace, we do not stand in our own righteousness but in the righteousness of Christ. Christ's sacrifice paid the penalty for sin completely: past, present, and future (Romans 3:21-26; 1 Corinthians 1:30; 2 Corinthians 5:21; Romans 4:6; 10:3-4; Philippians 3:9).

> "When I shall say to the righteous, that he shall surely live; if he trust to his own righteousness, and commit iniquity, all his righteousnesses shall not be remembered; but for his iniquity that he hath committed, he shall die for it" (Ezekiel 33:13).

Read also Ezekiel 33:7-9.

The warnings in Ezekiel 33:1-20 are very similar to those in Ezekiel 3. Read the notes on Ezekiel 3:20 above. The word of the fall of Jerusalem comes in verse 21 of Ezekiel 33. The warnings threaten physical death in the battle ahead if the people do not turn from their iniquity. Nothing is said of the loss of salvation or eternal punishment.

> "When the righteous turneth from his righteousness, and committeth iniquity, he shall even die thereby" (Ezekiel 33:18).

See the notes above on Ezekiel 3:20 and 33:13.

Here again physical death is stated as the result of sin but nothing is said of eternal salvation.

> "And I saw, when for all the causes whereby backsliding Israel committed adultery I had put her away, and given her a bill of divorce; yet her treacherous sister Judah feared not, but went and played the harlot also" (Jeremiah 3:8).

Read the context — Jeremiah 3:6-22.

This passage is written concerning a nation, not individuals. Eternal security applies to individuals.

> "For Israel slideth back as a backsliding heifer: now the LORD will feed them as a lamb in a large place" (Hosea 4:16).

> "And My people are bent to backsliding from Me: though they called them to the most High, none at all would exalt Him" (Hosea 11:7).

These passages concern the nation, Israel, not individuals and therefore the doctrine of eternal security does not apply.

> "Behold, all souls are Mine; as the soul of the father, so also the soul of the son is Mine: the soul that sinneth, it shall die" (Ezekiel 18:4).

Read all of Ezekiel 18, especially verse 20.

This passage is speaking of physical death as is obvious when the entire context is read. There is no loss of eternal life here.

This was under the law. Under grace, the one who is saved is already dead in the person of his substitute Jesus Christ (2 Corinthians 5:14; Galatians 2:20; Colossians 2:20; 3:3; 2 Timothy 2:11; Hebrews 2:9; Romans 6:6-8; 7:4; Galatians 2:19; Romans 6:13; Colossians 2:12-13; 3:1; Ephesians 2:4-6), and is free from the condemnation of the law. The sentence of death has already been carried out.

> "But he that receiveth the seed into stony places, the same is he that heareth the word, and anon with joy receiveth it; Yet hath he not root in himself, but dureth for a while: for when tribulation or persecution ariseth because of the word, by and by he is offended. He also that received seed among the thorns is he that heareth the word; and the care of this world, and the deceitfulness of riches, choke the word, and he becometh unfruitful" (Matthew 13:20-22).

Read also Matthew 13:1-23; Mark 4:1-20; and Luke 8:4-15.

Some say that this passage speaks of believers who are saved and then lost.

The seed in this parable is the Word of God (Luke 8:11). The Word of God is given out (sown). Some who hear are hardened and Satan catches away the Word lest it grow (the seed sown by the wayside — Matthew 13:4,19). Some who hear rejoice and appear outwardly to be saved but have no reality (no root). They profess to know the Lord but when persecution comes the truth is seen (the seed sown in stony places — Matthew 13:5-6,20-21). Some who hear are really saved and begin to grow but their love of worldliness stifles their growth and they never mature enough to win others (the seed that fell among thorns — Matthew 13:7,22). Some hear and believe and grow in the Lord and win others to Him (the seed that fell on good ground — Matthew 13:8, 23).

> "When the unclean spirit is gone out of a man, he walketh through dry places, seeking rest, and findeth none. Then he saith, I will return into my house from whence I came out; and when he is come, he findeth it empty, swept, and garnished. Then goeth he, and taketh with himself seven other spirits more wicked than himself, and they enter in and dwell there: and the last state of that man is worse than the first. Even so shall it be also unto this wicked generation" (Matthew 12:43-45).

Read also Luke 11:24-26.

This is an illustration of a person who has attempted to reform but has never really been born again. One who has been born again cannot be said to be an empty house for he is indwelt by the Holy Spirit (Romans 8:9) and the Holy Spirit will abide with him for ever (John 14:16-17). This passage shows how foolish it is to attempt to reform or try to live by the law apart from the new birth.

> "But he that shall endure unto the end, the same shall be saved" (Matthew 24:13).

Read also Matthew 10:22 and Mark 13:13.

Some say that we must "endure" in the sense of keeping our salvation until we die or that we will lose it.

The question here is what is meant by "endure" and what is meant by "saved." Nowhere in the Bible is salvation from the penalty of sin said to be brought about by "enduring." It is by believing. It is not of works. Kenneth Wuest writes: "That which is to be endured are the sufferings of the tribulation period. The end refers to the close of that period. Salvation here is not spiritual, for no one is ever saved by enduring anything, but is physical, physical protection and well-being for those who have endured the sufferings of that terrible period, these are saved to enter the millennium."[94]

The note in the New Scofield Bible says: "The reference is not to the salvation of the soul of the believer who endures persecution, but to his deliverance by the Lord's return."[95]

> "Then his lord, after he had called him, said unto him, O thou wicked servant, I forgave thee all that debt, because thou desiredst me: Shouldest not thou also have had compassion on thy fellow-servant, even as I had pity on thee? And his lord was wroth, and delivered him to the tormentors, till he should pay all that was due unto him. So likewise shall My heavenly Father do also unto you, if ye from your hearts forgive not every one his brother their trespasses" (Matthew 18:32-35).

Read the entire passage — Matthew 18:21-35.

This is under the law, but even here the servant was only to be tormented "till he should pay all that was due."

Under grace we are not servants but "sons." We are servants only as we serve voluntarily, because the love of Christ constraineth us. The principle of forgiveness under grace is: "Forgiving one another, even as God for Christ's sake hath forgiven you" (Ephesians 4:32). God "chastens" His sons but not by condemning them forever. He does so to bring them into conformity to His will "that we should not be condemned with the world" (1 Corinthians 11:32).

> "And when the king came in to see the guests, he saw there a man which had not on a wedding garment: And he saith unto him, Friend, how camest thou in hither not having a wedding garment? And he was speechless. Then said the king to the servants, Bind him hand and foot, and take him away, and cast him into outer darkness; there shall be weeping and gnashing of teeth" (Matthew 22:11-13).

These verses are in a parable about a king who prepared a

wedding (marriage feast) for his son (Matthew 22:1-14). The marriage feast represents the kingdom age which begins when Christ comes to earth again. The man without a wedding garment represents a man who is not clothed in the righteousness of Christ and is therefore lost. He is cast into the "outer darkness," that is, he is cast into the darkness that is outside the marriage feast (the kingdom). At the beginning of the kingdom all who are not "saved" are taken from the earth in judgment (Matthew 13:41,49; 3:12).

> "And while they went to buy, the bridegroom came; and they that were ready went in with him to the marriage: and the door was shut. Afterward came also the other virgins, saying, Lord, Lord, open to us. But he answered and said, Verily I say unto you, I know you not" (Matthew 25:10-12).

Read the entire passage — Matthew 25:1-13.

In this story told by Jesus some say that the five virgins who took no oil represent Christians who have lost their salvation.

Note carefully that they took "no oil" and that the Lord said, "I know you not." This parable looks forward to the second coming of Christ (the bridegroom). The marriage feast is the millennial age (the kingdom). The five foolish virgins took no oil. Oil is a symbol of the Holy Spirit, and "If any man have not the Spirit of Christ, he is none of His" (Romans 8:9). The Lord also says, "I know you not." This could never be said to any believer however unspiritual. Read also Matthew 7:21-23.

> "And cast ye the unprofitable servant into outer darkness: there shall be weeping and gnashing of teeth" (Matthew 25:30).

This verse is in a parable that looks ahead prophetically to the second coming of Christ (Matthew 25:14-30). The kingdom set up by Christ is a place of light and blessing. To be cast into the "outer darkness" means to be cast out of the kingdom into the darkness outside. It means death. See also note on Matthew 22:11-13.

The word "servant" does not always refer to those who are believers. All men have a responsibility to serve God for all are His creation. Even ungodly kings are called God's servants

(Jeremiah 25:9; 27:6; 43:10; Isaiah 44:28; 45:1).

The servant cast into the outer darkness in this parable represents an unbeliever who is on earth at the time of the Lord's second coming.

"Ye therefore, beloved, seeing ye know these things before, beware lest ye also, being led away with the error of the wicked, fall from your own stedfastness" (2 Peter 3:17).

"So, dearly beloved, since you have been forewarned, you must always be on your guard against being led astray by the errors of lawless men, and so against falling away from your present firmness" (2 Peter 3:17 Williams).

"fall from your own [present] firm condition — your own steadfastness [of mind]" (2 Peter 3:17b Amplified Bible).

Notice that it does not say that you "fall from your salvation" but from "your own stedfastness." The word translated "stedfastness" is used only here in the Greek New Testament and means "firm condition or stedfastness of mind." 96

A person may be saved and still not have steadfastness of mind.

"Wherefore let him that thinketh he standeth take heed lest he fall" (1 Corinthians 10:12).

"Therefore let anyone who thinks he stands — who feels sure that he has a steadfast mind and is standing firm — take heed lest he fall [into sin]" (1 Corinthians 10:12 Amplified Bible).

It is clear from the context that this is written to Christians about the possibility of falling, not from salvation, but into sin or a backslidden condition. There is nothing said about a loss of salvation.

"I am the true vine, and My Father is the husbandman. Every branch in Me that beareth not fruit He taketh away: and every branch that beareth fruit, He purgeth it, that it may bring forth more fruit. Now ye are clean through the word which I have spoken unto you. Abide in Me, and I in you. As the branch cannot bear fruit of itself, except it abide in the vine; no more can ye, except ye abide in Me. I am the vine, ye are the branches: He that abideth in Me, and I in him, the same bringeth forth much fruit: for without

Me ye can do nothing. If a man abide not in Me, he is cast forth as a branch, and is withered; and men gather them, and cast them into the fire, and they are burned" (John 15:1-6).

The problem in interpreting this passage is that it is an illustration and it is possible to stretch an illustration far beyond its intended meaning. The word "abide" when used of a Christian speaks of remaining in close fellowship with the Lord. To "abide in the vine," then, means unbroken fellowship with the Lord. To "abide not in the vine" speaks of broken fellowship. One who is not in close fellowship with the Lord will not produce fruit.

This passage is not written about our "standing" before God, for one who knows Christ as Saviour *now has everlasting life* (John 3:15-16,36; 5:24; 6:47; 10:28; 1 John 5:11-13) and *"shall never perish"* (John 10:28). It is written about our "state" for one who has everlasting life may not be living in close fellowship with the Lord. If we are living in broken fellowship with the Lord our witness to others will be worthless; it will be rejected and cast out by men.

We need the chastening and cleansing of the Lord even as the branches of the vine need the purging and cleansing of the vine-dresser.

The words in this passage were spoken by Jesus to His disciples (Judas had already left them) on the way to the garden of Gethsemane. He is emphasizing to them the need for remaining in close fellowship with Him.

In verse 2 He says, "Every branch in Me that beareth not fruit He taketh away." The word in the Greek which is translated "taketh away" (αἴρω) means to "lift up, raise, raise up, raise from the ground, take up, elevate." It means to "take away" only when additional words in the context clearly indicate this. The following will illustrate its usage: it is used of lifting up a bed — Matthew 9:6; Mark 2:3,9,11,12; Luke 5:24-25; John 5:8-12; of lifting stones — John 8:59; 11:39; of lifting a cross — Matthew 16:24; 27:32; Mark 8:34; 10:21; 15:21; of lifting a fish — Matthew 17:27; of lifting up a yoke — Matthew 11:29; of lifting baskets of food — Matthew 14:20; 15:37; Mark 6:43; 8:8,19-20; of picking up serpents — Mark 16:18; of lifting a corpse — Matthew 14:12; Mark 6:29; John 19:38. Notice especially the following, where it could not possibly mean "take away": it is used of lifting up a voice — Luke 17:13; Acts 4:24; of lifting up eyes — John 11:41; of lifting up a hand — Revelation 10:5. When the word means more than "lifting up" or "raising" it is clearly seen in the context, as in the following: Luke 8:12 *"taketh away* the word *out* of their hearts"; Matthew 22:13 *"take* him *away, and cast* him into [the] outer darkness"; Matthew 24:39 "the flood came, and *took* them all *away."*

The phrase in John 15:2 would be better translated, "Every branch in Me that beareth not fruit He lifteth up." There is no implication here that the branch is cut off and taken away but rather that it is lifted up, evidently from trailing on the ground that it may receive more sunlight and thus become fruitful.

The Lord goes on to say, "And every branch that beareth fruit, He purgeth it, that it may bring forth more fruit." The word here translated "purgeth" means to cleanse from filth and impurity. It is used in Hebrews 10:2 of worshipers being purged by sacrifices. They were "cleansed" by them.

A. W. Pink writes: "It may strike some of us as rather incongruous to speak of *cleansing* a branch of a vine. It would not be so if we were familiar with the Palestinian vineyards. The reference is to the washing off of the deposits of insects, of moss, and other parasites which infest the plant. Now the 'water' which the Husbandman uses in cleansing the branches is *the Word,* as verse 3 tells us. The thought, then, is the removal by the Word of what would obstruct the flow of the life and fatness of the Vine through the branches. Let it be clearly understood that this 'purging' *is not* to fit the believers for Heaven (that was accomplished, once for all, the first moment that faith rested upon the atoning sacrifice of the Lord Jesus Christ), but is designed to make us more fruitful, while we are here in this world."[97]

In verse 4 Jesus tells His disciples to "abide in" Him. To "abide" in Christ means to maintain unbroken fellowship and communion with Him. In so doing he will bring forth "much fruit" (verse 5). If a man does not "abide" in Christ, that is, he does not maintain fellowship and communion with Christ, he is "cast forth as a branch" (verse 6). This means that his fellowship with Christ is broken. Notice that what is illustrated here is not the eternal relationship of the believer to Christ but his fellowship and communion with Him.

Concerning the remainder of verse 6, A. W. Pink writes: "But what is meant by, 'Men gather them, and cast into the fire, and they are burned'? Observe, first, the plural pronouns. It is not 'men gather *him* and cast into the fire, and *he* is burned,' as it would most certainly have been had an unbeliever, a mere professor, been in view. The change of number here is very striking, and evidences, once more, the minute accuracy of Scripture. 'Unless any *one* abide in Me, he is cast forth as a branch, and men gather *them,* and cast into the fire, and *they* are burned.' The 'them' and the 'they' are *what issues* from the one who has been cast forth *'as* a branch.' And *what* is it that issues from such an one — what but *dead works:* 'wood, hay, stubble'! and what is to become of his 'dead works.' 1 Corinthians 3:15 tells us: 'If any man's work shall be *burned* (the very word used in John 15:6!), he shall suffer loss: but he himself shall be saved; yet so as by *fire.' Lot* is a pertinent example: he was out of fellowship with the Lord, he ceased to bear fruit to His glory, and his dead works were all burned up in Sodom; yet he himself was saved!"[98]

"If we confess our sins, He is faithful and just to forgive us our sins, and to cleanse us from all unrighteousness" (1 John 1:9).

Some say that we must keep confessing our sins in order to keep salvation.

This verse is certainly written to Christians but does not concern our eternal salvation but rather our lives now. As children of God we need to come to Him and confess our sins in order to continue in fellowship and communion with Him. If we do not confess our sins to Him we face the chastening of the Lord. In 1 Corinthians 11:31, in a passage speaking of chastening, it says, "For if we would judge ourselves, we should not be judged." Confession is a condition of fellowship and communion, not of salvation from the eternal penalty of sin.

"Let that therefore abide in you, which ye have heard from the beginning. If that which ye have heard from the beginning shall remain in you, ye also shall continue in the Son, and in the Father.

> And this is the promise that He hath promised us, even eternal life" (1 John 2:24-25).

The words "abide," "remain," and "continue" in verse 24 are all translations of the same Greek word (μένω). This word as used in the New Testament means "to sojourn, to tarry, to dwell at one's house, to tarry as a guest, to lodge, to maintain unbroken fellowship with one, to put forth constant influence upon one."[99] To "continue in the Son" means to have unbroken fellowship with Him. This is not written concerning the "standing" of a Christian but concerning his "state." His standing before God rests "in Christ" and does not change. However, his fellowship with God may be broken by sin.

> "He that hath an ear, let him hear what the Spirit saith unto the churches; He that overcometh shall not be hurt of the second death" (Revelation 2:11).

See also Revelation 2:7,17,26; 3:5,12,21 where the word "overcometh" is used in a similar way.

Some feel that these verses mean that a believer must do certain works or not do certain things in order to "overcome" or he will lose his salvation.

The real question here is what is meant by the word "overcometh"? The answer to this question is found in another book by the same author. 1 John 5:4-5 says: "For whatsoever is born of God overcometh the world: and this is the victory that overcometh the world, even our faith. *Who is he that overcometh the world, but he that believeth that Jesus is the Son of God?*"

"He that overcometh," then, is *every born-again believer.* These verses in Revelation 2 and 3 are really verses of security, for the things promised to "overcomers" are for all believers.

> "He that overcometh, the same shall be clothed in white raiment; and I will not blot out his name out of the book of life, but I will confess his name before My Father, and before His angels" (Revelation 3:5).

Some say that this verse implies that God may blot some names out of the book of life. However, the verse says nothing about blotting out any name but is a promise that He will *not* blot out the name of him "that overcometh." According to 1 John 5:4-5 "he that overcometh" is "he that believeth that Jesus is the Son of God."

This, then, is a verse of assurance for it is a promise to overcomers (all born-again believers) that God will not blot their names out of the book of life. Since God will not blot out their names they are eternally secure.

Why attempt to make the verse imply something that it does not say? In John 6:37 Jesus says: "Him that cometh to Me I will in no wise cast out." Are we to understand by this statement that Jesus is implying that He will cast out some who come to Him? Certainly not! Then why make Revelation 3:5 imply that He will blot out some names when our Lord here emphatically says that He "will not blot out his name out of the book of life"?

> "If any man's work shall be burned, he shall suffer loss: but he himself shall be saved; yet so as by fire" (1 Corinthians 3:15).

> "But if any person's work is burned up [under the test], he will suffer the loss (of it all, losing the reward), though he himself will be saved, but only as [one who has passed] through fire" (1 Corinthians 3:15 Amplified Bible).

> "If the structure which one builds is burned up, he will get no pay; and yet he himself will be saved; but just as one who goes through the fire" (1 Corinthians 3:15 Williams).

This is a passage that refers to the judgment seat of Christ. This is a judgment for Christians only. None at this judgment are lost for even those who "suffer loss" in this verse are saved. Christians' works are judged. Some receive rewards (1 Corinthians 3:14); some "suffer loss" of reward but all are saved.

> "Fear none of those things which thou shalt suffer: behold, the devil shall cast some of you into prison, that ye may be tried; and ye shall have tribulation ten days: be thou faithful unto death, and I will give thee a crown of life" (Revelation 2:10).

It is argued that only those who are faithful "unto death" will receive eternal life. This verse, however, does not say eternal life; it says "crown of life." The "crown of life" is one of the rewards given to Christians at the judgment seat of Christ (1 Corinthians 3:14, 2 Corinthians 5:10). Eternal life is a "free gift" (Romans 6:23; Ephesians 2:8-9).

"Behold, I come quickly: hold that fast which thou hast, that no man take thy crown" (Revelation 3:11).

Here as in the passage just discussed the "crown" does not refer to eternal life but to a reward given to Christians for faithful service. They are warned that they may lose a reward that could have been theirs because they neglect the truths that they have.

"But let a man examine himself, and so let him eat of that bread, and drink of that cup. For he that eateth and drinketh unworthily, eateth and drinketh damnation to himself, not discerning the Lord's body" (1 Corinthians 11:28-29).

The word "damnation" is an unfortunate translation for it seems to imply eternal punishment. The word "judgment" would be a better translation.

Williams translates: "eats and drinks a judgment on himself"

Amplified translates: "eats and drinks a sentence — a verdict of judgment — upon himself"

Wuest translates: "is eating and drinking so as to bring judgment upon himself."

What the judgment is, is shown in verse 30: "For this cause many are weak and sickly among you, and many sleep."

As we read on in verses 31 and 32 it becomes obvious that the judgment spoken of is God's "chastening" of His own. There is no threatened loss of salvation here.

"Having damnation, because they have cast off their first faith" (1 Timothy 5:12).

Here as in 1 Corinthians 11:29 the word translated "damnation" ($\kappa\rho\acute{\iota}\mu\alpha$) would be better translated "judgment." It refers to judgment taking place not in eternity but now in this life.

Wuest writes: "The word 'damnation' in A.D. 1611 was used in the sense of judgment or condemnation, as shown by the present tense of the participle 'having.' In its early usage, the word had in it no idea of a future punishment."[100] A.D. 1611 is the date when the King James version of the Bible was published.

"incurring [the reproachful] judgment [of their fellow Christians] because they have nullified their first faith" (1 Timothy 5:12 Wuest).

"and so deserve censure for breaking their previous pledge" (1 Timothy 5:12 Williams).

The passage is about the conduct of Christian widows, who may by their actions incur the judgment of others. There is no hint here of loss of salvation or of the eternal condemnation of God.

"But a certain man named Ananias, with Sapphira his wife, sold a possession, And kept back part of the price, his wife also being privy to it, and brought a certain part, and laid it at the apostles' feet. But Peter said, Ananias, why hath Satan filled thine heart to lie to the Holy Ghost, and to keep back part of the price of the land? Whiles it remained, was it not thine own? and after it was sold, was it not in thine own power? why hast thou conceived this thing in thine heart? thou hast not lied unto men, but unto God. And Ananias hearing these words fell down, and gave up the ghost: and great fear came on all them that heard these things" (Acts 5:1-5).

Read also Acts 5:6-11 concerning Sapphira.

We are given no reason to doubt that Ananias and Sapphira had really accepted the Lord. As believers, however, they committed a terrible sin with the result that they died. Physical death, however, does not mean they lost their salvation for even Christians living close to the Lord die.

In 1 Corinthians 11:30, because of disorder at the Lord's supper, Paul says, "For this cause many are weak and sickly among you, and many sleep." The death of a Christian is referred to as sleep (John 11:11-13; Acts 7:60; 1 Corinthians 15:6,18, 20,51; 1 Thessalonians 4:14; Matthew 27:52). God chastens His own when they disobey, even to calling them home to Heaven when they hinder His work (1 John 5:16).

"Then Simon himself believed also: and when he was baptized, he continued with Philip, and wondered, beholding the miracles and signs which were done. Now when the apostles which were at Jerusalem heard that Samaria had received the word of God, they sent unto them Peter and John: Who, when they were come down, prayed for them, that they might receive the Holy Ghost: (For as yet He was fallen upon none of them: only they were baptized in the name of the Lord Jesus.) Then laid they their hands on them, and they received the Holy Ghost. And when Simon saw that through laying on of the apostles' hands the Holy Ghost was given, he offered them money, Saying, Give me also this power, that on whomsoever I lay hands, he may receive the Holy Ghost. But Peter said unto him, Thy money perish with thee, because thou hast thought that the gift of God may be purchased with money. Thou hast neither part nor lot in this matter: for thy heart is not right in the sight of God. Repent therefore of this thy wickedness, and pray God, if perhaps the thought of thine heart may be forgiven thee. For I perceive that thou art in the gall of bitterness, and in the bond of iniquity" (Acts 8:13-25).

Some do not believe that Simon was really saved but that he only professed to believe. It is certainly possible for Christians to be fooled by the false profession of someone even to the point of baptizing that one. However, this does not appear to have been the case with Simon. The Bible does not say, "he professed to believe," but that he "believed."

If Simon was truly a believer he was yet a babe in Christ and had much to learn. He sought power in the wrong way and for the wrong purpose. John R. Rice writes: "So Simon, the ignorant new convert, carried over ideas from his profession in the past and offered to buy the right to give the Holy Ghost with the laying on of hands! The gift of God cannot be purchased with money. Salvation cannot be purchased by gifts of money, and no office in the church ought to be reward for liberal gifts."[101] How many Christians there are today who seek to be put into positions of importance for their own glory, or use their talents seeking the praise of men.

John R. Rice continues: "Peter said, 'Thy money perish with thee.' Money is temporal, material, and like Simon's body, would perish. The work of the Holy Spirit is intangible, spiritual, eternal."[102]

Simon's act would bring the chastening of God unless he

recognized his sin before God and judged it (1 Corinthians 11:31-32).

> "For Demas hath forsaken me, having loved this present world, and is departed unto Thessalonica; Crescens to Galatia, Titus unto Dalmatia" (2 Timothy 4:10).

We have no reason to question the salvation of Demas. He was, no doubt, saved. He is mentioned in Colossians 4:14 along with Luke as sending greetings to the Colossian Christians. In Philemon 24 he is mentioned along with Mark, Aristarchus, and Luke as Paul's fellow laborers. Demas had forsaken Paul. He was in a backslidden condition, out of fellowship and communion with God, but nothing is said here about his losing his salvation. A son may be very disobedient to his father and as a result find little fellowship with him but he is still his father's son. So also with a child of God.

All too often the pleasures of this world have lured Christians into lives of unfruitfulness.

> "If any man see his brother sin a sin which is not unto death, he shall ask, and he shall give him life for them that sin not unto death. There is a sin unto death: I do not say that he shall pray for it" (1 John 5:16).

Some who do not believe in the security of the believer use this verse to show that a believer may be lost, "sin a sin unto death." If this is the meaning, then there appears to be no hope for him. Believers are told not to pray for him. However, those who teach that believers may be lost urge Christians to pray for them.

There is obviously another meaning for this passage. This is a warning to Christians, not that their sin may bring about eternal death, for "they shall never perish" (John 10:28), but that sin may bring about physical death. This is not speaking of any particular sin. It would be better translated, "There is sin unto death." In 1 Corinthians 11 Paul speaks of some who "sleep" (are dead) because of misuse of the Lord's Supper. Ananias and Sapphira sinned unto death (Acts 5:1-11) but it does not say that they were lost. 1 John 5:18 shows that God will not let a Christian continually practice sin, and He may even call him home (to Heaven).

> "But I keep under my body, and bring it into subjection: lest that by any means, when I have preached to others, I myself should be a castaway" (1 Corinthians 9:27).

The meaning of this passage centers around the word translated "castaway." Nowhere else in the writings of Paul do we find any hint that Paul thought that there was any possibility that he might be lost. Instead there is the utmost confidence and assurance of salvation. What then does this mean? The word translated "castaway" means "disapproved." It is used in the writings of Paul's day to describe what was done with a cracked pot. It was not thrown away but was put on the shelf.[103] It is much the same as a baseball or football player being taken out of the game. He is not thrown off the team, but just put on the bench. Each one of us, then, who are in Christ, should work for God in such a way that we will not be put on the shelf.

The Greek word translated "castaway" is ἀδόκιμος. The opposite of this word is δόκιμος and means "approved." It is used in the following verses: Romans 14:18; 16:10; 1 Corinthians 11:19; 2 Corinthians 10:18; 2 Timothy 2:15; James 1:12.

> "Stand fast therefore in the liberty wherewith Christ hath made us free, and be not entangled again with the yoke of bondage. Behold, I Paul say unto you, that if ye be circumcised, Christ shall profit you nothing. For I testify again to every man that is circumcised, that he is a debtor to do the whole law" (Galatians 5:1-3).

Careful examination of the context will show that the "yoke of bondage" of which Paul speaks here is not a lost condition but rather the condition of being under the "law"; of attempting to keep the law as a necessity for salvation. Some, who do not believe in the security of the believer say that we are "saved by grace but kept by works." It is these very ones against whom Paul here argues, for they are attempting to put the Christian back under the law, "the yoke of bondage."

Lehman Strauss writes: "If the Galatians were to put themselves under law and submit to the rite of circumcision, they would deprive themselves of the effects of the ministry of the risen Christ. While their Christian standing before God would not be affected, their state would. If righteousness is sought through circumcision, or through any legal system, it cannot at the same time be received through Christ on the ground of grace. If salvation and justification and the promise of eternal life are obtained by the works of the law, then there was no need for God to send His Son to procure these blessings for us." [104]

In verse 3 Paul points out that if a man is seeking to be righteous by keeping the law, he must keep the whole law (and that is impossible).

> "Christ is become of no effect unto you, whosoever of you are justified by the law; ye are fallen from grace" (Galatians 5:4).

The words "ye are fallen from grace" are often quoted without the rest of this verse as proof that a believer may lose his salvation. When we look at the whole verse we realize that it is actually they themselves who insist upon works to remain saved who are said to have fallen from grace.[105] This passage is not speaking of those who have fallen into sin but rather those who are concerned with doing everything the law requires in order to be righteous. This verse does not say that they were once saved and then lost but rather that they have put themselves in a position under the law where grace is unable to work. Grace has already worked to bring about their salvation but is now unable to continue working (that is in teaching them how to live as Christians — Titus 2:11-12) because they are trying to put themselves back under the law rather than continuing "in the Spirit" (Galatians 3:3).

Galatians is not a treatise on the new birth or salvation from the penalty of sin but an appeal to life in the liberty of grace instead of bondage to the law.[106]

Concerning this passage, Kenneth S. Wuest writes: "These Judaizers came to the Galatian Christians who were truly regenerated, Spirit-indwelt children of God, and taught that they were justified by the Mosaic law (5:4). Because there was no such thing under the law as indwelling Holy Spirit, who had come to take up His permanent residence in the believer's heart for His ministry of sanctification, this teaching deprived these Galatian Christians of their dependence upon the Spirit, and thus also of the Spirit's work of manifesting Christ in outward expression in their lives (Acts 19:2). This is what Paul means when he says, 'ye are fallen from grace' (5:4). The apostle is not talking about their justification. The Holy Spirit had nothing to do with that. Justification is a purely legal matter. The entire context is that of sanctification and the work of the Spirit. He says, 'We through the Spirit wait for the hope of righteousness by faith' (5:5). He offers the cure for the condition in which they found themselves, in the words, 'Walk in the Spirit, and ye shall not fulfil the lust of the flesh' (5:16), and then speaks of the result of walking in the Spirit (verses 22 and 23). These Galatian Christians had fallen from grace in the sense that they had deprived themselves of the ministry of the Holy Spirit in which He ministered grace to them, daily grace for daily living (2 Corinthians 12:9; Galatians 5:4)."107

> "Therefore we ought to give the more earnest heed to the things which we have heard, lest at any time we should let them slip. For if the word spoken by angels was stedfast, and every transgression and disobedience received a just recompence of reward; How shall we escape, if we neglect so great salvation; which at the first began to be spoken by the Lord, and was confirmed unto us by them that heard Him" (Hebrews 2:1-3).

We cannot neglect our salvation until it is ours. This is evidently speaking of Christians who "neglect" their salvation. A man may be married and neglect his wife but she is still his wife. Christians do not lose their salvation by neglecting it but they do lose the joy and blessed fellowship that could be theirs.

Christians who "neglect" their salvation will be "chastened" of God (Hebrews 12:5-11; 1 Corinthians 11:32) in this life (receive a just recompence of reward — Hebrews 2:2) but will not be "condemned with the world."

> "Take heed, brethren, lest there be in any of you an evil heart of unbelief, in departing from the living God" (Hebrews 3:12).

This verse is evidently written to Christians. Nothing is said about a loss of salvation or about eternal punishment. It is a warning against backsliding. It is possible to "believe" and be saved from the penalty of sin, but then fail to enter into all the joy and blessing that could be ours as Christians because we don't fully believe that God means what He says. It is possible for born-again Christians to be "hardened through the deceitfulness of sin" (Hebrews 3:13).

Israel, nationally, belonged to the Lord and was and is eternally secure. God has not cast them out (Romans 11:1-6). But at Kadesh Barnea they failed to enter Canaan, their "rest," because of "unbelief" (Hebrews 3:7-19).

> "Let us therefore fear, lest, a promise being left us of entering into His rest, any of you should seem to come short of it" (Hebrews 4:1).

Read also the entire passage — Hebrews 4:1-16.

The "rest" for Israel was the land of Canaan. Canaan does not represent Heaven for it was still a place of conflict. Israel did not enter Canaan at Kadesh Barnea because of unbelief but they were still God's people. God did not cast them out, but because of unbelief they wandered in the wilderness for forty years instead of enjoying the blessings that could have been theirs in Canaan.

So it is with Christians today. Many who are really saved wander, as it were, in the wilderness not knowing the "rest" of God that could be theirs by believing. They fail to possess the blessings that are already theirs (Ephesians 1:3) because of unbelief.

> "For it is impossible for those who were once enlightened, and have tasted of the heavenly gift, and were made partakers of the Holy Ghost, And have tasted the good word of God, and the powers of the world to come, If they shall fall away, to renew them again unto repentance; seeing they crucify to themselves the Son of God afresh, and put Him to an open shame. For the earth which drinketh in the rain that cometh oft upon it, and bringeth forth herbs meet for them by whom it is dressed, receiveth blessing from God: But that which beareth thorns and briers is rejected, and is nigh unto cursing; whose end is to be burned" (Hebrews 6:4-8).

This is a passage often used by those who do not believe in the eternal security of the believer. Read carefully the entire passage and the verses following it. Do those who say that this passage teaches that a believer may be lost also say that those thus lost can never be renewed to repentance? They do not! They urge backsliders to come and be saved again. If this passage teaches that a believer may be lost it also teaches that he may never be saved again, for it says concerning those who fall away that it "is impossible ... to renew them again unto repentance."

There are three possible interpretations of this passage which we will present here:

Interpretation 1

This passage is hypothetical. That is, the writer here assumes something to be true in order to show that if it were true there would be certain results. Since the results cannot be, the original premise is shown to be false.

Paul uses this line of reasoning in 1 Corinthians 15:13-19 where he is speaking of the resurrection of the dead. He assumes that there is no resurrection in order to prove that there is.

If this is the case in this passage, then the writer is showing that if a believer could fall away it would be impossible to renew him to repentance, and since this certainly is not so then a believer cannot fall away.

Interpretation 2

This passage is speaking of those who have come to the very threshold of salvation but have turned back, "fallen away." They have "tasted" of the heavenly gift and the good Word of God, but tasting is not drinking. Jesus says that "whosoever drinketh of the water" (John 4:14) not whosoever "tasteth" of the water that He would give him would never thirst. We taste to see whether or not we will drink.

They "were made partakers of the Holy Ghost." No man can understand spiritual things unless the Spirit reveals them to him — "they are spiritually discerned" (1 Corinthians 2:14). Here then are some to whom the Holy Spirit has revealed the truth concerning salvation but after having known the truth they do not accept it but turn away. They deliberately reject the truth revealed to them by the Holy Spirit, and the Spirit ceases to work in their hearts.

They may be compared to a man who is walking in the darkness on a cold night. He comes to a door that is open and looks in. He can feel the warmth which is coming from inside but he does not enter. He "tasted" but he did not go in. Tasting or knowing the truth is not enough. One must accept it.

That this passage is not referring to Christians is obvious when we read Hebrews 6:9: "But, beloved, we are persuaded better things of you, and things that accompany salvation, though we thus speak." Those spoken of in this passage did not have "things which accompany salvation" so they could not have been saved.

Note also the change in person here. The "us" and "we" in verses 1 and 3 of chapter 6 change to "those" and "they" in verses 4 and 6 and to "we" and "you" in verse 9.

Interpretation 3

To my mind the best interpretation of this passage is that which holds that this is a warning to Christians that unless they go on to spiritual maturity, God may not let them. Not that they will lose their salvation but that they will lose the blessings and rewards that could have been theirs if they had only by faith claimed them, and that they will become unfruitful and produce works fit only to be burned.

Notice the context in which this passage is found. In chapter 3 of Hebrews we have an illustration of the children of Israel hardening their hearts and refusing to enter the promised land (Canaan) because of unbelief. God had promised to give them the land and to drive out the inhabitants from before them, but they refused to believe Him. Because of this God would not let them enter the land *even when they desired to do so* and they wandered for forty years until their "carcases fell in the wilderness" (Hebrews 3:17).

In chapter 4 the writer of Hebrews shows that there is a "rest" for believers, but that some may not enter into that rest because of unbelief. The land of Canaan is an illustration of that rest. Canaan does not illustrate Heaven, for even though it was a place of victory it was still a place of conflict. It illustrates for the believer that place of spiritual maturity where there is victory and blessing and rest.

In chapter 5 the writer of Hebrews points out to the believers that they need to grow up spiritually. There are many things that he would like to say to them but he cannot because they are still babes in Christ. This thought is continued into chapter 6 where he says in verse 1 that they should leave the basic things of the "doctrine of Christ" (the milk) and go on to "perfection" (spiritual maturity). In verse 3 he says, "And this we will do, *if God permit.*" There is, evidently, the possibility that God will not permit some to go on to spiritual maturity. Then follows the awful warning of verses 4-8.

Lance B. Latham writes: "The repentance that can no longer be effected is toward their perfection! These Christians, 'dull of hearing,' 'milk' Christians, 'babes' need this fearful warning — just as we need it today. There comes a time, in God's infinite knowledge and wisdom, when they cannot go on to perfection. 'It is impossible — to renew them again unto repentance' (not justification)." 108

God did not abandon the Israelites when He refused to let them enter Canaan but continued to watch over them and care for them. He continued to feed them with manna and to deliver them from their enemies. God will not abandon His own today even though He refuses them the blessings that could have been theirs if they had gone on to spiritual maturity.

Notice that those to which this passage refers:

"were once enlightened" (literally "once for all enlightened" — so translated by Wuest, Williams, Amplified, and others);

"have tasted of the heavenly gift";

"were made partakers of the Holy Ghost";

"have tasted the good word of God, and the powers of the world [age] to come."

It would certainly appear that those spoken of here are born-again Christians. *They have been "once for all enlightened."* The Greek word here translated "enlightened" ($\phi\omega\tau\acute{\iota}\zeta\omega$) is translated "illuminated" in Hebrews 10:32 where it refers to believers. They have seen the light of the gospel once for all.

They have "tasted" of the heavenly gift. They "tasted." This goes beyond the idea of just sampling salvation or coming to the threshold of salvation without really believing. The Greek word translated "tasted" in Hebrews 6:4 and 5 (γεύομαι) is the same word used in Hebrews 2:9 where it says concerning Jesus, "That He should taste death for every man." Did Jesus just sample death or did He enter thoroughly into it? The same word is translated "eat" in Acts 10:10; 20:11; 23:14. The word may also be translated "experience." "They have *experienced* the heavenly gift." "They have *experienced* the good word of God, and the powers of the world to come."

They "were made partakers of the Holy Ghost." The word translated "partakers" (μέτοχος) is also used in Hebrews 3:1: "partakers of the heavenly calling"; in Hebrews 3:14: "partakers of Christ"; and in Hebrews 12:8: "chastisement, whereof all are partakers." In Romans 8:9 it says, "if any man have not the Spirit of Christ, he is none of His."

They "tasted" or "experienced" the "powers of the world [age] to come." This implies that there had been at least some fruit in their lives as a result of the working of the Holy Spirit.

The word "if" in verse 6 is not in the Greek text and the verb used is a participle. The phrase translated, "If they shall fall away" in the King James Version would be better translated: "And falling away." Verse 6 does not state from what the believer is falling away. Therefore this must be determined by the context. The writer is speaking of going on to perfection (spiritual maturity) in verses 1 to 3 and this is evidently still the subject here (the "for" at the beginning of verse 4 ties the passages together). They are falling away from going on to spiritual maturity. The cares of this world are choking their fruitfulness.

"It is impossible ... to renew them again unto repentance." The word renew speaks of repetition. Williams translates: "It is impossible, I say, to keep on restoring them."

Lance B. Latham writes: "We must realize that the word

'repentance' is used — not salvation. The correct meaning of 'repentance' is 'change of mind.' It is used sometimes in reference to the unsaved — very often in reference to the saved. When the *unsaved* repent, the change of mind is invariably in connection with the Person and work of Christ — it is not reformation, or fresh law obedience. (It will pay you to check every use of this word in Acts and the Epistles, and verify the truth of this statement.) When the *saved* repent, their justification is in no way involved. The repentance of a believer for his misdeeds does not result in a fresh justification but in restoration. When a believer sins and does not repent, he fails to receive the restoration he needs — but his salvation, being a gift from God, remains unaffected. And besides, God will judge him here now (1 Corinthians 11:31-32). And he will lose out at the judgment seat of Christ (2 Corinthians 5:10)."[109]

There is evidently a point in the life of a Christian, who repeatedly refuses to go on to spiritual maturity, at which God will no longer allow him to go on to spiritual maturity even though he desires to do so, a point at which God will no longer allow him to have the blessings that could have been his if he had only fully believed. He is still the Lord's own and He will watch over him but he cannot enter into the rest illustrated by Canaan.

In Hebrews 12:16-17 Esau is given as an example of one who did not value his birthright and sold it for a morsel of meat (food). Because of this he lost out on the blessing that could have been his and "found no place of repentance, though he sought it ... with tears." Some Christians today do not really value their spiritual birthright and as a result of worldliness lose out on the blessing that could have been theirs and though they later seek it they find "no place of repentance."

In Hebrews 6:7-8 the writer uses the earth (soil) that "bringeth forth herbs" as an illustration of a Christian whose life is fruitful; and the earth (soil) which "beareth thorns and briers" to illustrate a Christian whose life is unfruitful but bears only that which is worthless. This is similar to two of the kinds of ground in the parable of the Sower (Matthew 13:1-23; Mark 4:1-25; Luke 8:4-15). The good ground brought forth much fruit (Matthew 13:23) but the ground with the thorns was unfruitful because of the "care of this world, and the deceitfulness of riches." See notes on this parable.

The soil bearing thorns and briers is "rejected, and is nigh unto cursing; whose end is to be burned." The word translated "rejected" (ἀδόκιμος)ι is the same word used by Paul in 1 Corinthians 9:27 and translated "castaway." It means to be disapproved. (See notes on 1 Corinthians 9:27.) It does not speak of a loss of salvation but of the loss of reward. Notice that Hebrews 6:8 does not say the "rejected" earth is cursed but that it is "nigh unto cursing." Read the passage in 1 Corinthians 3:12-15 about the testing of a Christian's works. It is parallel to Hebrews 6:7-8. Every Christian's works will be tried by "fire" (1 Corinthians 3:13). For that which remains the Christian receives a reward (1 Corinthians 3:14). If the work is burned he loses the reward that could have been his (1 Corinthians 3:15) but he is still saved, "yet so as by fire." Notice in Hebrews 6:8 the "end is to be burned." It is not the soil that burns but that which the soil produces — the thorns and briers. John 15:6 is another passage which speaks of the useless works of believers being burned. (See notes on John 15:1-6.)

Some who believe this passage (Hebrews 6:4-8) refers to the unsaved point to the change of person in the pronouns. The "us" and "we" of verses 1 and 3 change to "those and "they" in verses 4 and 6 and to "we" and "you" in verse 9. The reason for this is that the writer of Hebrews does not believe that those to whom he is writing have yet gone as far as those described in verses 4-6. He is "persuaded better things" of them (Hebrews 6:9), "and things that accompany salvation" (not salvation from the penalty of sin, which is past, but salvation, present tense, from the power of sin in their lives).

With the dreadful warning of Hebrews 6:4-8 in mind the writer in Hebrews 6:12 urges them not to be "slothful," "but followers of them who through faith and patience inherit the promises" for they are in danger of losing them through unbelief.

> "For if we sin wilfully after that we have received the knowledge of the truth, there remaineth no more sacrifice for sins" (Hebrews 10:26).

Read also Hebrews 10:27-34.

This passage is very similar to that which we have just discussed (Hebrews 6:4-8). We will present two possible interpretations of this passage:

Interpretation 1

Some hold that this passage refers to unbelievers. It says they have "received the knowledge of the truth." It does not say that they have accepted the truth and applied it to themselves. It is possible for one to know all about a bridge, for example, without crossing it. He may know about the man who designed it and know that it is a good bridge but until he crosses it, it does him no good.

William R. Newell writes: "There is no 'adversary' equal to a traitor — one who has enjoyed the privileges he now forsakes and betrays. Nor are we at all questioning the blessed doctrine of the security of Christ's sheep in what we say. Remember that in John's Gospel, both those eternally given by the Father to Christ (17:6,12), and those who were His disciples for a while and then 'went back, and walked no more with Him' (6:66) are seen. There is then a 'choosing' by Christ, and an association with Him, which may not mean eternally abiding in Him. So John 6:70 sets forth: 'Jesus answered them, Did not I *choose you twelve,* and one of you is a devil?' "110

Interpretation 2

We feel that the better interpretation of this passage is that it is speaking to Christians warning them of fearful consequences of willful sin, not loss of salvation, but chastening now in this life. Lance B. Latham lists several reasons for believing that those spoken of in this verse and those following are God's people:

"The contrast between 'we' (Hebrews 10:26) and 'the adversaries' (verse 27). These are two different classes. Also the penalty is different. There is a 'certain fearful looking for of judgment and fiery indignation,' for the 'we.' But this will 'devour' the adversaries.

"These addressed were 'sanctified' according to verse 29.

"Then notice — 'The Lord shall judge His people' verse 30. Not those who were once His people.

"They were not only believers, but had an unusually good testimony (verses 33 and 34).

"They knew that they had in Heaven a better and enduring substance! (verse 34)"[111]

Lance B. Latham continues by asking: *"What was their sin?* This would appear to be more than what is usually considered sin. For we have many passages where sin is dealt with, that carry every hope of forgiveness and reconciliation when judged. Note 1 Corinthians 11:31-32; 1 John 1:9 — much of 1 Corinthians and other passages.

"It would appear that these Jewish believers will turn back to Old Testament ceremonials and sacrifices. And in so doing, reject the one sacrifice offered once for all. In so doing, they would tread under foot the Son of God and count the precious blood an unholy thing and do despite to the Spirit of grace (Hebrews 10:29). The parallel would be the Gentile believer who turns his back on Christ as God's Son and on Calvary. Probably this is what would be called 'the willful sin.' There is no worse sin.

"We might add — with blatant denial of the Person of God's Son being taught in so-called Christian institutions today, many a true but immature believer is in danger of this very sin. With the approving recognition of liberals by holding meetings under their sponsorship, and parading them before the public as Christians, even having them lead in prayer — little wonder that many poorly instructed believers think that, after all, it makes little difference whether our Lord is insulted or not as to His birth and deity.

"This warning may well be applied to those who in any way make light of the absolute deity of the Lord Jesus.

"*The penalty* is fearful. In the case of a true believer, we do not believe eternal hell is the penalty. 'The adversaries' in verse 27 are *devoured;* the believer so ensnared has a 'certain fearful looking for of judgment and fiery indignation' — fearful enough, but not eternal hell.

"In the Old Testament, the one that despised Moses' law died without mercy under two or three witnesses. This was physical death. The punishment for the willful sin here is a 'sorer punishment than death' — the Word does not say, 'eternal loss.' Many punishments right here on earth could be sorer than death — a long continued disease, a cancer, etc."[112]

Lance B. Latham points out: "We have an extreme case in 1 Corinthians 5 of a believer who was guilty of unusually repulsive immorality. What was the penalty? Believers were to refuse him fellowship personally, and also fellowship in the church. But also — note — he was to be delivered to 'Satan for the destruction of the flesh, that the spirit may be saved in the day of the Lord Jesus' (1 Corinthians 5:5).

"Is there a like punishment for a believer guilty of blasphemy? There is. We find in 1 Timothy 1:19-20 — 'Holding faith, and a good conscience; which some having put [aside] concerning faith have made shipwreck; Of whom is Hymenaeus and Alexander; whom I have delivered unto Satan, that they may *learn not to blaspheme.'* Not that they may be damned — but may be taught a severe lesson, in all likelihood 'a sorer punishment than death.'

" *'There remaineth no more sacrifice for sins'* 1 John 1:9 — (along with 1 Corinthians 11:31-32) promises to believers forgiveness, and cleansing if they 'confess' ('judge') their sins. Here the blood cleanses. This does not refer to our justification, but to the cleansing of a believer. If we do not listen to God as His own, we do not receive the cleansing and family forgiveness, but must be judged.

'But when we are judged, we are chastened of the Lord, that we should not be condemned with the world!' (1 Corinthians 11:32)"[113]

Wuest translates Hebrews 10:26 as follows: "For if we go on sinning willfully after having received a full knowledge of the truth, no longer for sins does there remain a sacrifice."

"Cast not away therefore your confidence, which hath great recompence of reward" (Hebrews 10:35).

A Christian may lose his "confidence" without losing his salvation. Those who teach that Christians may lose their salvation are, by so doing, undermining the "confidence" of those they teach and are causing them to disregard the admonition here.

> "Now the just shall live by faith: but if any man draw back, My soul shall have no pleasure in him" (Hebrews 10:38).

> "Now My righteous person shall live by faith. But if he draw back in fear, My soul shall have no pleasure in him" (Hebrews 10:38 Wuest).

The one spoken of here is obviously a Christian. If one of the Lord's own draws back (backslides) he will be chastened by the Lord in His displeasure but he is not lost. The next verse shows this.

> "But we are not of them who draw back unto perdition; but of them that believe to the saving of the soul" (Hebrews 10:39).

> "But if thy brother be grieved with thy meat, now walkest thou not charitably. Destroy not him with thy meat, for whom Christ died" (Romans 14:15).

> "And through thy knowledge shall the weak brother perish, for whom Christ died?" (1 Corinthians 8:11)

Read also Romans 14:1-21 and 1 Corinthians 8:1-13.

Taken alone the two verses quoted above seem to say that a "brother" (evidently a Christian brother) can be lost. However, when the passages are examined carefully the true meaning is seen. Romans 14:21 explains what is meant by "destroy" in Romans 14:15.

> "It is good neither to eat flesh, nor to drink wine, nor any thing whereby thy brother stumbleth, or is offended, or is made weak" (Romans 14:21).

1 Corinthians 8:12-13 explains what is meant by 1 Corinthians 8:11. The "weak conscience" of the brother is "wounded" and he is made to "offend." It does not say that he is lost.

John 10:28 clearly says concerning the Lord's own that "they shall never perish."

Wuest's translation of Romans 14:15 and 1 Corinthians 8:11 is good:

> "For, if because of food your brother is made to grieve, no longer are you conducting yourself according to love. Stop ruining by your food that one on behalf of whom Christ died" (Romans 14:15 Wuest).

> "For the one who is weak, through your knowledge is being ruined [in his Christian life], your brother on account of whom Christ died" (1 Corinthians 8:11 Wuest).

The words "destroy" and "perish" imply more in our present day English than is meant here. There is no thought in either Romans 14:15 or 1 Corinthians 8:11 of a Christian losing his salvation but rather of his life as a Christian being hindered and his spiritual growth stymied.

> "Beloved, believe not every spirit, but try the spirits whether they are of God: because many false prophets are gone out into the world" (1 John 4:1).

Read the entire passage — 1 John 4:1-6.

The false prophets referred to here are not saved ones who have lost their salvation but who never had salvation to begin with. Nothing is said of their losing their salvation. They are obviously unsaved for "they are of the world" (1 John 4:5).

> "For such are false apostles, deceitful workers, transforming themselves into the apostles of Christ. And no marvel; for Satan himself is transformed into an angel of light. Therefore it is no great thing if his ministers also be transformed as the ministers of righteousness; whose end shall be according to their works" (2 Corinthians 11:13-15).

Here as in the passage above nothing is said about these "false apostles" ever having been saved. They are said to be Satan's ministers (verse 15). They are merely pretenders.

"But there were false prophets also among the people, even as there shall be false teachers among you, who privily shall bring in damnable heresies, even denying the Lord that bought them, and bring upon themselves swift destruction" (2 Peter 2:1).

Here again, as in the two passages above, nothing is said about these "false teachers" ever really knowing the Lord. Read all of 2 Peter 2 and it will be obvious that these are unsaved.

"And if any man shall take away from the words of the book of this prophecy, God shall take away his part out of the book of life, and out of the holy city, and from the things which are written in this book" (Revelation 22:19).

The Greek manuscripts do not say "*book* of life" but rather "*tree* of life." The word translated "tree" in Revelation 22:2 of the King James Version is the same word here translated "book."

"God shall take away his part from the tree of life" (New American Standard and the New Scofield Bible)

"God will subtract from him his share in the tree of life" (Williams).

"God will cancel and take away from him his share in the tree of life" (Amplified Bible).

"God shall take away his portion from the tree of life" (Wuest).

The one spoken of here has never been saved and has never had his name in the book of life and so will not be allowed in the Holy City where the "tree of life" is (Revelation 22:2), and will, therefore, have no part in the "tree of life." (See note on Revelation 3:5.)

"If any man defile the temple of God, him shall God destroy; for the temple of God is holy, which temple ye are" (1 Corinthians 3:17).

The words "defile" and "destroy" in this verse are both translations of the same Greek word. If the word "destroy" is speaking of eternal destruction, as some claim, then the word "defile" must also mean eternal destruction and this doesn't make sense. Some idea of what is meant by the word translated "destroy" and "defile" is seen when we realize that "in the opinion of the Jews the Temple was corrupted or 'destroyed,' when any one defiled or in the slightest degree damaged anything in it, or if its guardians neglected their duties."[114]

Nothing is said here about the loss of salvation. It is in effect saying that "whatsoever a man soweth, that shall he also reap" (Galatians 6:7).

> "Well; because of unbelief they were broken off, and thou standest by faith. Be not highminded, but fear: For if God spared not the natural branches, take heed lest He also spare not thee" (Romans 11:20-21).

Read also all of Romans 11.

The natural branches are the Jews. They were broken off because of unbelief (Romans 11:20). Through their "fall" salvation is offered to the Gentiles (Romans 11:12). The warning here is to the Gentiles. It is not a warning to individual believers that they will be cast out.

William R. Newell writes: "Some, who deny the eternal safety of the saints, apply the warning of verses 20-21, as if it were a personal, instead of a generic one — a warning to individual believers, instead of to Gentiledom as such. But this is not only bad theology, but missing of Paul's whole point here. It is bad theology, for our Lord says of His sheep, that they 'shall never perish' and when Paul warns believers of being 'highminded' (compare 1 Timothy 6:17 with Romans 11:20) it is not to threaten doom to them, but to counsel them how to walk. Then, it is bad interpretation: for the whole passage in Romans 11:19-24, deals not with the Church (where there is no distinction between Jew and Greek!), but with Jew-position and Gentile-position in God's affairs on earth. Israel, unbelieving, was cut off for a while from his place of divine favor and blessing. Gentiledom comes into favor instead of Israel, for a while; and 'the Church came into the administration of the promises in the character of Gentiles, in contrast with Jews.' It is to a characteristic Gentile, that Paul speaks in Romans 11:19: 'Thou wilt say ... Branches were broken off, that I might be grafted in.' He speaks generically, to this characteristic Gentile, when he warns, in verse 22: 'Toward thee, [God's] goodness, if thou continue in His goodness: otherwise thou also shalt be [as was Israel before Gentiledom] cut off.' Now we know, from God's prophetic Word, that Gentiledom will, indeed, be cut off, as was Israel, and Israel be restored to his former place, as the sphere and channel of God's blessing to earth."[115]

"Remember therefore from whence thou art fallen, and repent, and do the first works; or else I will come unto thee quickly, and will remove thy candlestick out of his place, except thou repent" (Revelation 2:5).

This is not written to an individual Christian but to a local church, the church at Ephesus. The candlestick (lampstand) represents the church (Revelation 1:20) giving out the light of the gospel. This church is warned that the Lord will remove its candlestick. It will cease to be His church. It may continue in the eyes of men as a church but it will not be God's church.

Ephesus eventually lost its candlestick. It ceased to really be God's church, and so has many a gospel preaching church since, because of compromise and laxity; because of allowing unsaved people to become members, allowing them eventually to become the majority and control the church.

Eternal security applies to individual believers, not local churches.

"And unto the angel of the church of the Laodiceans write; These things saith the Amen, the faithful and true witness, the beginning of the creation of God; I know thy works, that thou art neither cold nor hot: I would thou wert cold or hot. So then because thou art lukewarm, and neither cold nor hot, I will spue thee out of My mouth. Because thou sayest, I am rich, and increased with goods, and have need of nothing; and knowest not that thou art wretched, and miserable, and poor, and blind, and naked: I counsel thee to buy of Me gold tried in the fire, that thou mayest be rich; and white raiment, that thou mayest be clothed, and that the shame of thy nakedness do not appear; and anoint thine eyes with eyesalve, that thou mayest see" (Revelation 3:14-18).

This is a warning, not to an individual believer, but to a local church, the church at Laodicea. At the time of this warning unbelievers were evidently the majority in this church for spiritually it was "wretched, and miserable, and poor, and blind, and naked." The church is counseled to buy "white raiment" (the righteousness of Christ). As a church the Lord says He will "spue" them out of His mouth.

At the close of this letter from the Lord to the church at Laodicea He makes an appeal to individuals:

> "Behold, I stand at the door, and knock: if any man hear My voice, and open the door, I will come in to him, and will sup with him, and he with Me" (Revelation 3:20).

Even though the church is to be spued out individuals who believe may be saved. Eternal security does not apply to local churches but to individual believers.

> "Moreover, brethren, I declare unto you the gospel which I preached unto you, which also ye have received, and wherein ye stand; By which also ye are saved, if ye keep in memory what I preached unto you, unless ye have believed in vain" (1 Corinthians 15:1-2).

Nowhere in the Bible is anyone said to be saved from the eternal penalty of sin by keeping anything in memory, but by believing. Salvation from the penalty of sin is spoken of as an already accomplished fact for the believer, not as a process now going on. However, the believer is being saved from the power of sin as a continuing process in his life.

1 Corinthians 15:1-2 presents salvation in the past *and* present tenses. In 1 Corinthians 15:1 Paul says that he is making known to them the gospel which he preached, which they had received (past tense, Greek — aorist, active, indicative), and in which they stood. This shows that they were already saved from the penalty of sin. In 1 Corinthians 15:2 he goes on to the present tense of salvation, "By which also ye are saved" (literally "are being saved" — Greek — present, passive, indicative — indicating action now going on). They are "being saved" from the power of sin, that is, they are growing in grace, maturing as

Christians, "if they were keeping in memory (holding fast)" what Paul preached to them.

They did not have the New Testament as we do and through which we "grow" spiritually, so they grew as Christians by remembering the words of those God sent to preach to them. When we do not read God's Word or hear it preached we do not grow as Christians; so with those at Corinth, if they did not "keep in memory" that which Paul had preached they would not grow as Christians.

1 Corinthians 15:2 ends with the statement, "unless ye have believed in vain." In other words, unless their belief was "unreal" — unless they had never really been saved.

> "Now, I am making known to you, brethren, the good news which I brought as glad tidings to you, which also you took to yourselves, in which also you have taken a stand, through which you are being saved, in what word I announced it to you as glad tidings, assuming that you are holding it fast unless you believed in vain" (1 Corinthians 15:1-2 Wuest).

> "Wherefore, my beloved, as ye have always obeyed, not as in my presence only, but now much more in my absence, work out your own salvation with fear and trembling" (Philippians 2:12).

Here again salvation is referred to in the present tense as something now going on. Whenever the Bible speaks of salvation from the eternal penalty of sin it is spoken of for the believer as an already accomplished fact, as completed (Ephesians 2:5,8; 2 Timothy 1:9).

"Salvation" is God's great inclusive term. It includes all that God has ever done for sinful man, all He is doing, and all He will do for eternity. Believers have already been eternally saved from the penalty of sin. They are now being saved from the power of sin in their daily lives (growing in grace). Some day they will be saved from the very presence of sin when Jesus comes again.

When Paul says "work out your own salvation," he is writing to Christians urging them to mature spiritually. This is the present tense of salvation — salvation from the power of sin.

Kenneth S. Wuest writes: "There is no idea here of an unsaved person doing good works to earn salvation, and for two reasons; first, because those addressed were already saved, and second, because the Bible is clear in its teaching that 'Not by works of righteousness which we have done, but according to His mercy He saved us' (Titus 3:5). Again, the passage does not mean that a Christian should work out an inworked salvation. There is no such idea in the Greek.

"The English translation is good, if one uses the words 'work out' as one does when referring to the working out of a problem in mathematics, that is, carrying it to its ultimate goal or conclusion. The Greek word here means just this.

"The words 'your own salvation,' are to be taken in their context. The working out of the Philippians' salvation was affected in some way by the presence of Paul with them and his absence from them. When Paul was with them, his teaching instructed them, his example inspired them, his encouragement urged them on in their growth in grace. Now in his absence they were thrown upon their own initiative. They must learn to paddle their own canoe. Thus Paul sets before them their human responsibility in their growth in grace, for sanctification is in the apostle's mind. They have their justification. Their glorification will be theirs in eternity. Their growth in Christ-likeness is the salvation concerning which Paul is speaking. Thus, the saints are exhorted to carry their growth in grace to its ultimate goal, Christ-likeness. 1 John 3:2 speaks of the saint's future conformation to the image of Christ, and (3:3) says, 'And every man that hath this hope set on Him purifieth himself, even as He is pure.' "[116]

> "Take heed unto thyself, and unto the doctrine; continue in them: for in so doing thou shalt both save thyself, and them that hear thee" (1 Timothy 4:16).

Here again we see salvation in the present tense. (See notes on Philippians 2:12.) This is not talking about salvation from the penalty of sin but of salvation from the power of sin. Timothy was already saved but continuing in sound doctrine he would grow spiritually and help those to whom he preached to grow spiritually.

> "While I was with them in the world, I kept them in Thy name:

those that Thou gavest Me have I kept, and none of them is lost, but the son of perdition; that the scripture might be fulfilled" (John 17:12).

Some say that this verse shows that Judas was once saved but that he lost his salvation. Jesus, however, says that *He* kept those that the Father had given Him. They did not keep themselves — *He* kept them. In John 6:39 Jesus says: "And this is the Father's will [who] hath sent Me, that of all [that] He hath given Me I should lose nothing, but should raise it up again at the last day."

In John 18:9 we read: "That the saying might be fulfilled, which He spake, Of them [whom] Thou gavest Me have I lost none."

There are no exceptions listed in these verses. None of those that the Father gave to Jesus were lost. Judas was never given to Jesus by the Father. He was never one of His own. God in His infinite foreknowledge knew all about Judas before the foundation of the world.

Early in His ministry Jesus pointed out that there were some of them that "believed not" and the Bible says that He knew this "from the beginning ... and who should betray Him" (John 6:64). In John 6:70-71 Jesus says that one of the twelve was a "devil." Judas never really believed. Judas was chosen as one of the twelve, not as one to be saved. Jesus knew very well that Judas would betray Him even before He chose him.

In John 17:12 Judas is not listed as an exception to those Jesus had kept but in contrast to them. None of those the Father gave to Jesus was lost, but Judas was lost.

The same construction in the Greek is used in Matthew 12:4:

"How he [David] entered into the house of God, and did eat the shew bread, which was not lawful for him to eat, neither for them which were with him, but only for the priests?"

The priests were not an exception to the ones listed but in contrast to them.

Dr. H. A. Ironside writes: "You may be sure that whenever

the Father gives any one to Jesus, He gives him for time and eternity. Such an one will never be lost. 'Being confident of this very thing that He which hath begun a good work in you will perform it until the day of Jesus Christ.' People call this the doctrine of the perseverance of the saints, but I rather like to think of it as the perseverance of the Saviour. He says, 'Those that Thou gavest Me I have kept.' If I had to keep myself, I would be hopeless of getting through. I would be sure that something would happen some day which would cause me to lose my hold on Christ and be lost. But it is His hold upon me on which I rely. None can pluck the believer out of His hand. I receive great comfort from these words. When He gives His account to the Father, when the last believer of this dispensation is safely arrived in Heaven, He will be able to say of the entire elect Church, 'Those that Thou gavest Me I have kept, and none of them is lost.' You may think you know of exceptions to this; but it will be made manifest in that day that these apparent exceptions were like Judas himself, never really born of God."[117]

> "That he may take part of this ministry and apostleship, from which Judas by transgression fell, that he might go to his own place" (Acts 1:25).

Concerning this verse John R. Rice writes: "Notice that it was 'part of this ministry and apostleship, fromwhich Judas by transgression fell.' He fell from an official position. It is not hinted that he fell from salvation."[118]

Rice asks: "Does it seem strange that an unsaved man would be allowed to go with Jesus as an apostle? Remember that the betrayal by Judas was foretold in the Old Testament and that is referred to by Peter in Acts 1:16 and 20.

"Besides, Judas was typical of many, many others in all ages who have 'a form of godliness without the power thereof' (2 Timothy 3:5). Jesus warned us that there would be many such. In Matthew 7:15 He warned, 'Beware of false prophets, which come to you in sheep's clothing, but inwardly they are ravening wolves.' In Matthew 7:21-23 He said: 'Not every one that saith unto Me, Lord, Lord, shall enter into the kingdom of heaven; but he that doeth the will of My Father which is in heaven. Many will say to Me in that day, Lord, Lord, have we not prophesied in Thy name? and in Thy name have cast out devils? and in Thy name done many wonderful works? And then will I profess unto them, I never knew you: depart from Me, ye that work iniquity.'

"And Jude 4 warns us of 'ungodly men, turning the grace of our God into lasciviousness, and denying the only Lord God, and our Lord Jesus Christ.' It should not be surprising, then, that Judas is typical of thousands of others unconverted in the churches, even in places of leadership in churches who are unconverted sinners deceiving and being deceived, blind leaders of the blind."[119]

"From that time many of His disciples went back, and walked no more with Him" (John 6:66).

The word translated "disciple" means "a follower, a pupil, a learner." One may follow without reality. These followed Jesus until He said things they didn't like. Notice that the passage does not say that they lost their salvation but that they "walked no more with Him." Even true believers may backslide and walk out of fellowship with the Lord but loss of fellowship is not the loss of salvation.

"Therefore, brethren, we were comforted over you in all our affliction and distress by your faith: For now we live, if ye stand fast in the Lord" (1 Thessalonians 3:7-8).

Notice it says, "now *we* live," not, "now *ye* live."

To say that this passage implies that Paul's salvation could be lost if the believers at Thessalonica did not stand fast is utterly contrary to all other Scriptures. Paul is not speaking of eternal life here but of the blessings and joy in his life now as a result of knowing of their "standing fast." Williams translates this verse: "For now I am really living since you are standing firm in the Lord."

"Fight the good fight of faith, lay hold on eternal life, whereunto thou art also called, and hast professed a good profession before many witnesses" (1 Timothy 6:12).

Paul here is writing to Timothy encouraging him in his life as a Christian. He tells him to "fight the good fight of faith." The word "fight" is that which was used of the Greek athletic games. *Expositor's Greek Testament* translates this phrase, "Engage in the contest."[120] In 2 Timothy 4:7 Paul says, "I have fought a good fight."

In 1 Timothy 6:12 Paul continues by saying, "lay hold on eternal life" (take possession of). Kenneth S. Wuest writes: "Now, when Paul exhorts Timothy to lay hold of eternal life, he does not imply that he does not possess it. Timothy was saved, and possessed eternal life as a gift of God. What Paul was desirous of was that Timothy experience more of what this eternal life is in his life."[121] Eternal life is ours spiritually from the moment we truly believe (John 3:36; 5:24), but we need to enter by faith into its blessings now, in this life.

H. A. Ironside writes: "So eternal life is the present portion of all believers. What does the apostle mean, then, when he says, 'Lay hold on eternal life'? It is an exhortation to make it a practical thing as we go through this scene. It is quite possible to trust in Christ and thus to have eternal life in the soul, and yet to drop down to a low spiritual level where one is not living in the reality of eternal life. He exhorts everyone of us to enter into that life which is unworldly and heavenly in character. When in this scene, Christ Himself was the manifestation of eternal life. It is a poor thing to talk about having eternal life while living for the things of the world. 'Lay hold on eternal life!' As I realize that my life is hid with Christ in God I will look very lightly upon the things of this world. Its pleasures will not attract me; its treasures will not possess my soul. I can go through this world as using without abusing the things God gives me. Knowing Him, whom to know is life eternal, everything else is of little importance. Thus one may lay hold on eternal life."[122]

"Laying up in store for themselves a good foundation against the time to come, that they may lay hold on eternal life" (1 Timothy 6:19).

The word "eternal" is not in the best manuscripts.

"in order that they may lay hold of that which is truly life" (Wuest).

"so that they may grasp that which is life indeed" (Amplified Bible).

The thought here is much the same as that in 1 Timothy 6:12. We need to experience in our lives now the blessings that come from eternal life.

H. A. Ironside writes: "The exact rendering should be 'that they may lay hold on that which is *really* life.' You see, the rich man imagines, when he enjoys all the pleasures that his wealth can give him, that he is seeing life, that he is having a good time. As he passes his hours in pleasure he says, 'This is life!' The apostle says that this is not life at all; that is just death. If you want to see life, if you want to enjoy life at its very best, then use what God has committed to your trust for the blessing of others. If you really want to be happy, and you are sure you know the Lord, if you have come to Him and taken your place before Him as a lost, guilty sinner, and trusted Him as your Saviour, you have passed from death unto life — then I can tell you what to do, not on my own authority, but as it is given here in the Word of God: begin today, and use what God has given you for the blessing of others; try to think of people in need who could be benefited by what you have hoarded away, Ask God to guide you as to using your money to the good of others that you may be rich in good works. If a man is rich only in stocks, bonds, and real estate, when he dies he will have to leave it all behind; but if he is rich in good works, when he dies he will take these with him — that is treasure laid up in Heaven. Be ready to distribute when opportunity is given; to use of your means for furthering the work of the Lord, assisting the needy, helping the lepers, relieving the blind, and caring for orphans. Be ready to give; do not hold back or say, 'Oh, well; I suppose I ought to do it.' Be glad that God has enabled you to help, and be willing to communicate. If you use your money in that way you will be laying up in store a good foundation against the time to come, for this is real life."[123]

"But if, while we seek to be justified by Christ, we ourselves also are found sinners, is therefore Christ the minister of sin? God forbid. For if I build again the things which I destroyed, I make myself a transgressor. For I through the law am dead to the law, that I might live unto God" (Galatians 2:17-19).

"But if, in our desire and endeavor to be justified in Christ — to be declared righteous and put in right standing with God wholly and solely through Christ — we have shown ourselves sinners also and convicted of sin, does that make Christ a minister (a party and contributor) to our sin? Banish the thought! — Of course not! For if I [or any other] — who have taught that the observance of the Law of Moses is not essential to being justified by God, should now by word or practice teach or intimate that it is essential — building up again what I tore down, I prove myself a transgressor. For I through the Law — under the operation [of the curse] of the Law — have [in Christ's death for me] myself died to the Law and all the Law's demands upon me, so that I may [henceforth] live to and for God" (Galatians 2:17-19 Amplified Bible).

Concerning this passage Lehman Strauss writes: "In paraphrase Paul says: 'If after we have accepted Christ as Saviour (which we did, seeking to be justified) we are still unsaved and in our sins, then Christ is the promoter of sin in getting us to abandon the law, and His promises are untrue. But away with any idea like that. Such a thought is preposterous!'

"At the sacrifice of his own life Paul had fought to show the Gentiles blameless apart from their keeping any Jewish ceremonial rite. To attempt to restore now what he had torn down would be folly and would prove him to be a transgressor (Galatians 2:18). This he could not do since he was now 'dead to the law' since the law had convicted and executed him. Since he was dead to the law he was no longer under its authority. He could now 'live unto God' (verse 19)." [124]

"Follow peace with all men, and holiness, without which no man shall see the Lord" (Hebrews 12:14).

The word here translated "holiness" (ἁγιασμός) is the same word that is translated "sanctification" in several places. The believer stands "in Christ" and in Him (Christ's) holiness or sanctification is counted as the believer's (1 Corinthians 1:30). William R. Newell writes: "All those who are *in Christ* are 'sanctified.' This is seen from 1 Corinthians 1:2, 'the Church of God which is at Corinth, [even] them that are *sanctified in Christ Jesus.*' This cannot refer to their 'experience,' for we see from 1 Corinthians 3:1-3 that they were 'babes' and 'carnal.' But they were no longer in Adam, but in the Second Man, Christ, and

2 Corinthians 5:17 was true of them — they were 'new creatures.' "[125] In Hebrews 10:10 we see that "we are sanctified
through the offering of the body of Jesus Christ once for all."

Therefore we who believe already have "holiness" or
"sanctification." In Hebrews 12:14 we are told to "follow ...
holiness." This means that we should seek, through yielding to
the Holy Spirit, to make true in our daily lives that which is
already true of us in our eternal standing before God.

> "Looking diligently lest any man fail of the grace of God; lest
> any root of bitterness springing up trouble you, and thereby many
> be defiled" (Hebrews 12:15).

> "Continue to look after one another that no one fails to gain
> God's spiritual blessing, or some evil like a bitter root may spring
> up and trouble you, and many of you be contaminated by it"
> (Hebrews 12:15 Williams).

All who truly believe have been saved "by grace" once for all
and therefore stand saved today. (See notes on Ephesians 2:8-9.)

After we have been saved by grace, grace continues to work,
teaching us to live "soberly, righteously, and godly" (Titus 2:11-
12). It is possible for one who has been saved by grace to sin and
lead others into sin and therefore fail to let grace teach him.
Nothing is said here of a loss of salvation.

> "And you, that were sometime alienated and enemies in your
> mind by wicked works, yet now hath He reconciled in the body of
> His flesh through death, to present you holy and unblameable and
> unreproveable in His sight: If ye continue in the faith grounded
> and settled, and be not moved away from the hope of the gospel,
> which ye have heard, and which was preached to every creature
> which is under heaven; whereof I Paul am made a minister"
> (Colossians 1:21-23).

Some say that salvation is ours only "if" we "continue in the
faith." The words in the Greek here translated "if" are used in a
way that indicates certainty — "of a thing believed to be
correctly assumed"[126] (εἴγε) with the present indicative — see
Ephesians 3:2; 4:21; 2 Corinthians 5:3). This passage is not
looking to the future but is speaking of the Christian's present
condition as a test of the reality of his salvation — "If it is now a

2

fact that you are (at this present time) abiding in the faith."
There is no threat of the loss of salvation here.

> "But Christ as a son over His own house; whose house are we, if
> we hold fast the confidence and the rejoicing of the hope firm unto
> the end" (Hebrews 3:6).

Some say that this verse teaches that we can lose our
salvation if we do not "hold fast."

Notice that the verse does not say, "whose house we will
continue to be, if we hold fast," but "whose house we are (now)
(present tense) if...." The holding fast demonstrates that we
are His house. This is a proof that we *are* saved, a test of the
reality of our salvation.

> "For we are made partakers of Christ, if we hold the beginning
> of our confidence stedfast unto the end" (Hebrews 3:14).

> "for we have become participators of Messiah and as a present
> result are participators of Him, [and that is shown] if we hold the
> beginning of our assured expectation steadfast to the end"
> (Hebrews 3:14 Wuest).

This verse is very similar to Hebrews 3:6. It presents a test
of the reality of our salvation. Notice that it does not say, "we will
continue to be partakers of Christ, if we hold" but rather "we are
made (Greek — perfect, active, indicative) partakers of Christ,
if we hold ...." Wuest, in his translation quoted above, brings out
the Greek more clearly — action that has been completed in the
past with present results. Holding "the beginning of our confidence stedfast unto the end" is proof that we are now saved.

> "Brethren, if any of you do err from the truth, and one convert
> him; Let him know, that he which converteth the sinner from the
> error of his way shall save a soul from death, and shall hide a
> multitude of sins" (James 5:19-20).

Concerning this passage H. A. Ironside writes: "The sinning
one here, as in verse 15 above, is a believer who has gone astray
from the path of subjection to the truth. To patiently go after such
an one and to convert, or turn him again, to obedience to the Lord
is to save a soul from death — physical death which is the last act

of God in His government of His family — and to cover or hide a multitude of sins. This is to practice that charity which Peter also tells us 'shall cover the multitude of sins' (1 Peter 4:8), not our own sins of course, but those of the erring brother. By leading him to repentance, so that he judges himself and acknowledges his waywardness, he is restored to fellowship with God and preserved from going deeper into sin, so that the heavy hand of the Lord should not have to be upon him in further chastening, even to shortening his life on earth as an evidence of the divine displeasure. This is the same as sinning unto death in 1 John 5:16-17. Many a child of God has been taken Home far earlier than he would otherwise have been, because of willfulness and insubjection of spirit." [127]

"Wherefore the rather, brethren, give diligence to make your calling and election sure: for if ye do these things, ye shall never fall" (2 Peter 1:10).

This is, in effect, saying, "make sure you are saved."

"Election" is of God and He elected (chose) us before the foundation of the world (Ephesians 1:4). Therefore if we are truly saved we have been elected (chosen) of God. Our election *is* sure. The question is, "Are we truly saved?" If an "elect one" could be lost then God made a mistake in choosing him.

The words "these things" evidently refer back to the same things which are mentioned as "these things" in 2 Peter 1:8-9 and listed in 2 Peter 1:3-7: "if ye do these things, ye shall never fall" — not from salvation, but into being "barren" and "unfruitful" (2 Peter 1:8).

"Now the Spirit speaketh expressly, that in the latter times some shall depart from the faith, giving heed to seducing spirits, and doctrines of devils; Speaking lies in hypocrisy; having their conscience seared with a hot iron; Forbidding to marry, and commanding to abstain from meats, which God hath created to be received with thanksgiving of them which believe and know the truth" (1 Timothy 4:1-3).

These spoken of here have departed from the faith held by their fathers. "There is no reference here to personal faith." [128] Kenneth S. Wuest writes: "The definite article before the word 'faith' marks it out as speaking, not of faith as an act, but of the Faith, that body of doctrine which forms the basis of what we as Christians believe."[129]

This passage does not say that they once believed and then departed. It is obvious that they themselves never believed for they are contrasted at the end of verse 3 with "them which believe and know the truth." Today we don't have to look far to find many who are doing the very things described here: "forbidding to marry, and commanding to abstain from meat."

> "For if after they have escaped the pollutions of the world through the knowledge of the Lord and Saviour Jesus Christ, they are again entangled therein, and overcome, the latter end is worse with them than the beginning. For it had been better for them not to have known the way of righteousness, than, after they have known it, to turn from the holy commandment delivered unto them" (2 Peter 2:20-21).

Here it speaks of a "knowledge" of Christ, but it does not say that they have received Him. Knowledge is not enough. One must apply that knowledge to himself and accept Christ's payment for sin. Knowledge cannot, in itself, save a man.

M. R. DeHaan writes: "If you have been reared in a Christian home, and been taught the knowledge of Jesus from your infancy, and been religious, you will escape much of the outward pollution of this world. But unless you are born again, it will not avail. There are thousands of fine, moral, lawabiding, sober, religious church members who have never been saved. A child can be raised to be religious and moral, and later turn his back upon the church and father's instructions, and live in filth and corruption. But what does that prove? It certainly does not prove that he was a Christian, and is now lost. On the contrary, it proves that he never was saved."[130]

The next verse should be quoted with this passage:

> "But it is happened unto them according to the proverb, The dog is turned to his own vomit again; and the sow that was washed to her wallowing in the mire" (2 Peter 2:22).

It is easy to understand how the dog would return to its vomit.

It was still a dog. The washed sow would return to the mire because she was still a sow. The nature of these animals remained the same. A Christian, however, is nowhere in the Bible called a "dog" or a "sow." He is a "new creature." He has a new nature. He will not continually return to the things which once he loved for he has been born again. He may slip into sin, driven by the devil, but he will not be happy in sin for he has a new nature.

H. A. Ironside writes: "Charles H. Spurgeon well said on one occasion, 'If that dog or that sow had been born again and had received the nature of a sheep it never would have gone back to the filth here depicted.' The dog is used as a symbol of false teachers on more than one occasion in Scripture. The sow is the natural man who may be cleansed outwardly but still loves the hog-wallow, and as soon as restraint is off he will go back to the filth in which he once lived."[131]

> "From which some having swerved have turned aside unto vain jangling" (1 Timothy 1:6).

> "Some people have stepped aside from these things and turned to fruitless talking" (1 Timothy 1:6 Williams).

This is evidently speaking of Christians who have been led by false teachers into fruitlessness. Nothing is said about their losing their salvation.

H. A. Ironside writes: "He (Paul) stresses the need of preaching the Word, the importance of this gospel of Christ which is the sole remedy for sin. Some had swerved from this and had turned aside unto vain jangling, because false teachers had gotten into the church, and some were not strong enough to resist them and so were carried away by their specious theories. They had swerved from the simplicity that is in Christ. It is ever the object of the devil to obscure the truth and get Christians occupied with something that will hide the glorious face of the Lord Jesus Christ, and becloud the truth regarding His finished work."[132]

> "Holding faith, and a good conscience; which some having put away concerning faith have made shipwreck: Of whom is Hymenaeus and Alexander; whom I have delivered unto Satan, that they may learn not to blaspheme" (1 Timothy 1:19-20).

It is possible to be shipwrecked and live, as was true of Paul several times. Hymenaeus and Alexander are given as examples of some who have made shipwreck concerning the faith. Paul says that he delivered them "unto Satan" not that they might be lost but that they might "learn not to blaspheme." This is speaking of the "chastening" of a Christian. It is similar to what is said concerning the believer at Corinth who was involved in deep immorality and Paul says that the Corinthians should "deliver such an one unto Satan for the destruction of the flesh, that the spirit may be saved in the day of the Lord Jesus" (1 Corinthians 5:5). Satan is allowed, under the permissive will of God, to bring physical suffering to Christians who are out of God's will.

> "And their word will eat as doth a canker: of whom is Hymenaeus and Philetus; Who concerning the truth have erred, saying that the resurrection is past already; and overthrow the faith of some" (2 Timothy 2:17-18).

Here are two men, evidently Christians, who were teaching false doctrine. Hymenaeus is mentioned also in 1 Timothy 1:20. It is possible for a Christian to be led astray into false doctrine and even to teach it. He will certainly be chastened of the Lord but it does not say that he will lose his salvation. The next verse (2 Timothy 2:19) points out that the Lord knows them that are His. We may have a hard time telling the difference between one who "professes" to be saved and one who really is, but the Lord knows and will keep His own.

> "For the love of money is the root of all evil: which while some coveted after, they have erred from the faith, and pierced themselves through with many sorrows" (1 Timothy 6:10).

The context in which this verse is found is a passage on Christian conduct. The love of money can hinder the life of a Christian and cause broken fellowship with God. As a result God chastens His own and sorrows come in this life. Nothing, however, is said here of eternal punishment or of the loss of salvation.

> "Wherefore come out from among them, and be ye separate, saith the Lord, and touch not the unclean thing; and I will receive you" (2 Corinthians 6:17).

It is argued from this verse that God will receive only those who come out and "be separate."

However, this appeal for a separated life is based on the previous verse (the "therefore" points back to it) and this verse states that we are the temple of the living God. This verse (17) then is an appeal to holy living based on the security of the believer and not a threatened loss of salvation. The last phrase of the verse carries this out. "I will receive you." There is no "if" or condition here.

> "If we say that we have fellowship with Him, and walk in darkness, we lie, and do not the truth: But if we walk in the light, as He is in the light, we have fellowship one with another, and the blood of Jesus Christ His Son cleanseth us from all sin" (1 John 1:6-7).

The subject here is fellowship, not salvation. When we cease to "walk in the light" our fellowship with the Lord and other Christians is broken but our salvation is not lost. If we do not confess our sins as Christians and judge them we will be chastened of the Lord (1 John 1:9; 1 Corinthians 11:31-32).

The communion and fellowship of a believer depends upon his attitude toward the Lord and his behavior; but his relationship with God depends upon his birth (new birth).

> "If we suffer, we shall also reign with Him: if we deny Him, He also will deny us" (2 Timothy 2:12).

Some say this verse means that if we deny that we know Him, He will deny He knows us and we will be lost. The word "deny," however, as used here means to withhold. "If we deny Him" (withhold) our service, our fellowship, our lives, He will deny us (withhold from us) the blessings and joy and fellowship that could have been ours.

REFERENCE NOTES

1. DeHaan, *Eternal Security*, p.21.
2. Carroll, *The Eternal Safety and Security of All Blood Bought Believers*, p.4.
3. Strombeck, *Shall Never Perish*, p.22.
4. *Ibid.*, p.25.
5. *Ibid.*, p.25.
6. Ironside, *In the Heavenlies* [*Ephesians*], pp. 112-113.
7. Wuest, *The New Testament — An Expanded Translation*, p.451.
8. ----. *Golden Nuggets from the Greek New Testament*, p.39.
9. Strombeck, *Shall Never Perish*, pp. 25-26.
10. *Ibid.*, pp.28-29.
11. *Ibid.*, p.29.
12. Newell, *Romans Verse by Verse*, p.412.
13. *Ibid.*, p.127.
14. Carroll, *The Eternal Safety and Security of All Blood Bought Believers*, p.4.
15. *New Scofield Reference Bible*, p.1276 note.
16. Carroll, *The Eternal Safety and Security of All Blood Bought Believers*, p.18.
17. *New Scofield Reference Bible*, p.1126 note.
18. Strombeck, *Shall Never Perish*, pp.45-46.
19. Mackay, *Grace and Truth*, p.45.
20. *Ibid.*, p.46.
21. Walvoord, *The Holy Spirit*, p.133.
22. *Ibid.*, p.137.

174   *Secure Forever*

23. Carroll, *The Eternal Safety and Security of All Blood Bought Believers*, p.12.
24. Mackay, *Grace and Truth*, pp.47-48.
25. *Ibid.*, p.48.
26. DeHaan, *Eternal Security*, p.7.
27. Newell, *Hebrews Verse by Verse*, p.245.
28. Ironside, *Hebrews and Titus*, pp.90-91.
29. Strombeck, *Shall Never Perish*, p.75.
30. *Ibid.*, p.76.
31. DeHaan, *Eternal Security*, p.18.
32. Strombeck, *Shall Never Perish*, p.183.
33. Newell, *Hebrews Verse by Verse*, p.341.
34. Strombeck, *Shall Never Perish*, p.34.
35. Nicoll, *The Expositor's Greek Testament*, vol. IV, pp.157-158.
36. Strombeck, *Shall Never Perish*, p.5.
37. Mackay, *Grace and Truth*, p.27.
38. Strombeck, *Shall Never Perish*, p.38.
39. DeHaan, *Dead to the Law*, p.2.
40. Strombeck, *Shall Never Perish*, pp.41-42.
41. DeHaan, *Dead to the Law*, p.4.
42. Newell, *Hebrews Verse by Verse*, p.343.
43. *Ibid.*, p.343.
44. *Ibid.*, p.405.
45. Strombeck, *Shall Never Perish*, p.68.
46. *Ibid.*, p.68.
47. Culbertson, *God's Provision for Holy Living*, p.33.
48. DeHaan, *Election — Predestination and Free Will*, p.15.
49. ----. *Eternal Security*, p.12.
50. Strombeck, *Shall Never Perish*, p.55.
51. Newell, *Romans Verse by Verse*, p.333.
52. *Ibid.*, p.338.
53. DeHaan, *Eternal Security*, p.16.
54. Newell, *Romans Verse by Verse*, p.376.
55. Ironside, *In the Heavenlies (Ephesians)*, p.78.
56. Strauss, *Galatians and Ephesians*, p.128.

57. Chafer, *Salvation*, p.125.
58. Strombeck, *Shall Never Perish*, pp.73-74.
59. Walvoord, *The Holy Spirit*, pp.158-159.
60. Mackay, *Grace and Truth*, p.90.
61. Chafer, *Salvation*, p.125.
62. Gordon, *In Christ*, p.20.
63. *Ibid.*, p.17.
64. *Ibid.*, p.39.
65. DeHaan, *Dead to the Law*, p.13.
66. Newell, *Romans Verse by Verse*, pp.104-105.
67. *Ibid.*, p.114.
68. *Ibid.*, p.114.
69. *Ibid.*, p.105.
70. *Ibid.*, p.99.
71. *Ibid.*, p.100.
72. Ironside, *Full Assurance*, p.25.
73. Strombeck, *Shall Never Perish*, p.86.
74. Adapted from Newell, *Romans Verse by Verse*, p.448.
75. Strombeck, *Disciplined by Grace*, p.91.
76. ----. *Shall Never Perish*, pp.101-102.
77. *Ibid.*, p.104.
78. *Ibid.*, pp.87-88.
79. *Ibid.*, pp.98-99.
80. Chafer, *Salvation*, p.112.
81. *Ibid.*, p.113.
82. DeHaan, *Eternal Security*, p.19.
83. Ironside, *In the Heavenlies* (*Ephesians*), p.117.
84. Newell, *Romans Verse by Verse*, p.236.
85. Gordon, *In Christ*, p.23.
86. *Ibid.*, p.43.
87. Strombeck, *Shall Never Perish*, pp.13-14.
88. DeHaan, *Eternal Security*, p.22.
89. Strombeck, *Shall Never Perish*, pp.113-114.
90. *Ibid.*, p.114.
91. *Ibid.*, p.112.
92. *Ibid.*, p.116.

93. *Ibid.*, p.143.
94. Wuest, *Mark in the Greek New Testament*, pp.248-249.
95. *New Scofield Reference Bible*, p.1034 note.
96. Thayer, *Greek-English Lexicon of the New Testament*, p.588.
97. Pink, *Gospel of John*, vol. III, p.295.
98. *Ibid.*, pp.303-304.
99. Wuest, *Studies in the Vocabulary of the Greek New Testament*, p.64.
100. ----. *The Pastoral Epistles in the Greek New Testament*, p.83.
101. Rice, *Filled with the Spirit — The Book of Acts*, p.193.
102. *Ibid.*, p.193.
103. Strombeck, *Shall Never Perish*, pp.149-151.
104. Strauss, *Galatians and Ephesians*, p.75.
105. Strombeck, *Shall Never Perish*, pp.146-147.
106. *Ibid.*, p.147.
107. Wuest, *Untranslatable Riches from the Greek New Testament*, p.77.
108. Latham, *Hebrews*, p.36.
109. *Ibid.*, p.38.
110. Newell, *Hebrews Verse by Verse*, p.355.
111. Latham, *Hebrews*, p.53.
112. *Ibid.*, pp.53-54.
113. *Ibid.*, p.54.
114. Thayer, *Greek-English Lexicon of the New Testament*, p.652.
115. Newell, *Romans Verse by Verse*, pp.422-423 note.
116. Wuest, *Golden Nuggets from the Greek New Testament*, pp.69-70.
117. Ironside, *Gospel of John*, pp.754-755.
118. Rice, *Filled with the Spirit — The Book of Acts*, p.59.
119. *Ibid.*, p.60.
120. Nicoll, *The Expositor's Greek Testament*, vol. IV, p.145.

121. Wuest, *The Pastoral Epistles in the Greek New Testament,* p.98.

122. Ironside, *Timothy, Titus, and Philemon,* pp.147-148.

123. *Ibid.,* pp.153-155.

124. Strauss, *Galatians and Ephesians,* p.31.

125. Newell, *Hebrews Verse by Verse,* p.410.

126. Thayer, *Greek-English Lexicon of the New Testament,* p.111.

127. Ironside, *James and Peter,* pp.62-63.

128. Chafer, *Salvation,* p.100.

129. Wuest, *The Pastoral Epistles in the Greek New Testament,* p.66.

130. DeHaan, *Eternal Security,* p.30.

131. Ironside, *James and Peter,* pp.90-91.

132. Ironside, *Timothy, Titus, and Philemon,* p.21.

BIBLIOGRAPHY

Carroll, J. M. *The Eternal Safety and Security of All Blood Bought Believers.* Indianapolis, Indiana, Claude King, Sr., 1960.

Chafer, Lewis Sperry. *Salvation.* Grand Rapids: Dunham Publishing Company, 1967.

Culbertson, William. *God's Provision for Holy Living.* Chicago: Moody Press.

DeHaan, M. R. *Dead to the Law.* Grand Rapids: Radio Bible Class.

----. *Election — Predestination and Free Will.* Grand Rapids: Radio Bible Class.

----. *Eternal Security.* Grand Rapids: Radio Bible Class.

Gordon, A.J. *In Christ.* Grand Rapids: Baker Book House, 1964.

Ironside, H.A. *Addresses on the Gospel of John.* Neptune, New Jersey: Loizeaux Brothers, 1942.

----. *Addresses on Timothy, Titus, and Philemon.* Neptune, New Jersey: Loizeaux Brothers, 1947.

----. *Expository Notes on the Epistles of James and Peter.* Neptune, New Jersey: Loizeaux Brothers, 1947.

----. *Full Assurance.* Chicago: Moody Press.

----. *In the Heavenlies (Ephesians).* Neptune, New Jersey: Loizeaux Brothers, 1937.

----. *Studies in the Epistle to the Hebrews and the Epistle to Titus.* Neptune, New Jersey, Loizeaux Brothers, 1932.

Latham, Lance B. *Hebrews.* Woodworth, Wisconsin: Brown Gold Publications.

Mackay, W. P. *Grace and Truth.* Abr. ed. Chicago: Moody Press (Moody Colportage Library, 458).

New Scofield Reference Bible. New York: Oxford University Press, 1967.

Newell, William R. *Hebrews Verse by Verse.* Chicago: Moody Press, 1947.

----. *Romans Verse by Verse.* Chicago: Moody Press, 1945.

Nicoll, W. Robertson. *The Expositor's Greek Testament.* Grand Rapids: Wm. B. Eerdmans.

Pink, Arthur W. *Exposition of the Gospel of John.* Grand Rapids: Zondervan, 1945.

Rice, John R. *Filled with the Spirit — The Book of Acts.* Murfreesboro, Tennessee: Sword of the Lord, 1963.

Strauss, Lehman. *Devotional Studies in Galatians and Ephesians.* Neptune, New Jersey: Loizeaux Brothers, 1957.

Strombeck, J. F. *Disciplined by Grace.* Chicago: Moody Press, 1946 (Moody Colportage Library 370).

----. *Shall Never Perish.* 8th ed. Moline, Illinois: Strombeck Agency, 1956.

Thayer, Joseph Henry. *Greek-English Lexicon of the New Testament.* New York: American Book Company, 1889.

Walvoord, John F. *The Holy Spirit.* Findlay, Ohio: Dunham Publishing Company, 1958.

Wuest, Kenneth S. *Golden Nuggets from the Greek New Testament.* Grand Rapids: Wm. B. Eerdmans, 1960.

----. *Mark in the Greek New Testament.* Grand Rapids: Wm. B. Eerdmans, 1950.

----. *The New Testament — An Expanded Translation.* Grand Rapids: Wm. B. Eerdmans, 1962.

----. *The Pastoral Epistles in the Greek New Testament.* Grand Rapids: Wm. B. Eerdmans, 1960.

----. *Studies in the Vocabulary of the Greek New Testament.* Grand Rapids: Wm. B. Eerdmans, 1962.

----. *Untranslatable Riches from the Greek New Testament.* Grand Rapids: Wm. B. Eerdmans, 1959.

ACKNOWLEDGMENTS

I gratefully acknowledge the following, who have granted me permission to quote from the books and booklets mentioned:

American Baptist Board of Education and Publication, Valley Forge, Pennsylvania
>Montgomery, Helen Barrett: *The New Testament in Modern English*

Baker Book House, Grand Rapids, Michigan
>Gordon, A. J.: *In Christ*

Brown Gold Publications, Woodworth, Wisconsin
>Latham, Lance B.: *Hebrews*

Wm. B. Eerdmans Publishing House, Grand Rapids, Michigan
>Nicoll, W. Robertson: *Expositor's Greek Testament*, vol. IV
>Wuest, Kenneth S.: *Golden Nuggets from the Greek New Testament*
>----. *Mark in the Greek New Testament*
>----. *The New Testament — An Expanded Translation*
>----. *The Pastoral Epistles in the Greek New Testament*
>----. *Studies in the Vocabulary of the Greek New Testament*
>----. *Untranslatable Riches from the Greek New Testament*

Claude King, Sr., Indianapolis, Indiana
>Carroll, J. M.: *The Eternal Safety and Security of All Blood Bought Believers*

The Lockman Foundation, La Habra, California
>*Amplified New Testament*, Zondervan Publishing House
>*New American Standard Bible — New Testament*, Moody Press

Moody Press, Chicago, Illinois
>Culbertson, William: *God's Provision for Holy Living*

Mackay, W. P.: *Grace and Truth*
Newell, William R.: *Hebrews Verse by Verse*
----. *Romans Verse by Verse*
Strombeck, J. F.: *Disciplined by Grace*
Williams, Charles B.: *The New Testament*

Oxford University Press, New York,
   New Scofield Reference Bible

Radio Bible Class, Grand Rapids, Michigan
   DeHaan, M. R.: *Dead to the Law*
   ----. *Election — Predestination and Free Will*
   ----. *Eternal Security*

Strombeck Foundation, Moline, Illinois
   Strombeck, J. F.: *Shall Never Perish*

Sword of the Lord, Murfreesboro, Tennessee
   Rice, John R.: *Filled with the Spirit*

Zondervan Publishing House, Grand Rapids, Michigan
   Chafer, Lewis Sperry: *Salvation*
   Pink, Arthur W.: *Exposition of the Gospel of John, vol. III*
   Walvoord, John F. *The Holy Spirit*

SCRIPTURE REFERENCE INDEX

182